Anthony Keefe

Not Quite All There

A collection of short homilies

Blessed Hope Publishing

Impressum / Imprint
Bibliografische Information der Deutschen Nationalbibliothek: Die Deutsche Nationalbibliothek verzeichnet diese Publikation in der Deutschen Nationalbibliografie; detaillierte bibliografische Daten sind im Internet über http://dnb.d-nb.de abrufbar.
Alle in diesem Buch genannten Marken und Produktnamen unterliegen warenzeichen-, marken- oder patentrechtlichem Schutz bzw. sind Warenzeichen oder eingetragene Warenzeichen der jeweiligen Inhaber. Die Wiedergabe von Marken, Produktnamen, Gebrauchsnamen, Handelsnamen, Warenbezeichnungen u.s.w. in diesem Werk berechtigt auch ohne besondere Kennzeichnung nicht zu der Annahme, dass solche Namen im Sinne der Warenzeichen- und Markenschutzgesetzgebung als frei zu betrachten wären und daher von jedermann benutzt werden dürften.

Bibliographic information published by the Deutsche Nationalbibliothek: The Deutsche Nationalbibliothek lists this publication in the Deutsche Nationalbibliografie; detailed bibliographic data are available in the Internet at http://dnb.d-nb.de.
Any brand names and product names mentioned in this book are subject to trademark, brand or patent protection and are trademarks or registered trademarks of their respective holders. The use of brand names, product names, common names, trade names, product descriptions etc. even without a particular marking in this work is in no way to be construed to mean that such names may be regarded as unrestricted in respect of trademark and brand protection legislation and could thus be used by anyone.

Coverbild / Cover image: www.ingimage.com

Verlag / Publisher:
Blessed Hope Publishing
ist ein Imprint der / is a trademark of
OmniScriptum GmbH & Co. KG
Heinrich-Böcking-Str. 6-8, 66121 Saarbrücken, Deutschland / Germany
Email: info@blessedhope-publishing.com

Herstellung: siehe letzte Seite /
Printed at: see last page
ISBN: 978-3-639-50076-9

Copyright © 2015 OmniScriptum GmbH & Co. KG
Alle Rechte vorbehalten. / All rights reserved. Saarbrücken 2015

NOT QUITE ALL THERE

By Anthony Keefe

TABLE CONTENTS

PREFACE…………………………………………………………………	4
Waking and walking…………………………………………………..	5
Wackiness for the Kingdom…………………………………………..	7
Patience with the provisional…………………………………………	9
The unsung hero………………………………………………………	11
Journey into danger…………………………………………………..	13
YOU are the Beloved…………………………………………………	15
The servant who takes away sin………………………………………	17
Get a move on! ……………………………………………………….	19
Light for a darkened world……………………………………………	21
Love rules, but don't love rules………………………………………	23
There's the rub……………………………………………………….	25
Worried? Who's worried? ……………………………………………	27
Water, water, everywhere…………………………………………….	29
Do you see what I see? ………………………………………………	31
Dead or alive………………………………………………………….	33
A homily for Holy Thursday…………………………………………	35
An Easter homily…………………………………………………….	37
Seeing and believing…………………………………………………	39
We are the Young Ones………………………………………………	41
Smelly sheep…………………………………………………………	43
How special are you? ………………………………………………..	45
Breaking the rules……………………………………………………	47
Don't talk rubbish! …………………………………………………..	49
Did you receive the Spirit? …………………………………………..	51
A homily for Corpus Christi………………………………………….	53
Flawed geniuses—Saints Peter and Paul…………………………….	55
The pierced heart…………………………………………………….	57
What kind of soil? ……………………………………………………	59
A puzzle from Paul…………………………………………………..	61
Tell us about the Kingdom……………………………………………	63
Loaves and fishes…………………………………………………….	65
Courage in the storm…………………………………………………	67
No to anti-Semitism………………………………………………….	69
There are answers and answers………………………………………	71
Tell me what you want……………………………………………….	73
Who wants a fight? …………………………………………………..	75
The bite of the serpent………………………………………………..	77
What time is it? ………………………………………………………	79
To be the same as Christ Jesus……………………………………….	81
What do you know about vines? …………………………………….	83
Remember, remember... …………………………………………….	85
The Lateran Basilica? Eh? ………………………………………….	87

Ye ken the noo! 89

PREFACE

The title of this short book requires a degree of explanation. This is a collection of homilies preached in the churches of St. Thomas the Apostle, Claughton-on-Brock, and Saints Mary and James, Scorton, both in the Roman Catholic Diocese of Lancaster, in the course of a year. They do not cover every weekend or Feast of that year, for a number of reasons. During a couple of weekends, I was on holiday; on other occasions, there may have been a Mission Appeal in the parishes; some homilies I felt did not lend themselves to publication. To that extent, they are "not quite all **there**".

There is, though, a second reason for the title. Over thirty years ago, during my first spell as chaplain to Our Lady's High School (now Our Lady's Catholic College) Lancaster, I was stopped in the corridor by a lad from the Fifth Year (Year 11 in new money).

"My mum thinks you are a right laugh" he said.

"Oh" I replied. "I didn't know I knew your mum."

"Well, you don't," came the response, "but I told her about your assemblies, and she thinks you are a right laugh. She said DO YOU THINK HE IS ALL THERE?"

"Thanks a bunch!" I retorted. "I don't know your mum, and you give her the idea that I am barmy. Great!"

But then I thought about it. Didn't St. Paul claim that we are "fools for the sake of Christ"?, So perhaps as Christians we are supposed to be "not quite all there". Maybe this lad's mum had it right, all those years ago. As you read these more recent offerings, you can judge for yourself, and also consider whether you too can take pride in being a fool for the sake of the Master.

I should, perhaps, add one thing. These homilies were delivered by a Roman Catholic priest to Roman Catholic congregations, so there may sometimes be allusions or assumptions which are unfamiliar to non-Roman Catholics. Nonetheless, I hope that there may still be enough to strike chords for Christians of other traditions, and even for the interested enquirer.

Reflection 1

Is.2:1-5, Ps.12:1-9, Rom. 13:11-14, Matt.24:37-44

Waking and walking

Where are we going, and what sort of state are we in? Some say that we are going to hell in a handcart; others that we are sleepwalking into the future. Isaiah envisaged the nations making a pilgrimage to Jerusalem—to the Temple—where their arrival would signal universal peace and harmony. This would mark the Reign or Kingdom of God, which Jesus told us, had begun through His coming in our human flesh.

Well, if it has begun, where is it? Do we see God reigning over nations which have put away the weapons of war? Do we heck as like! Indeed "Judaea and Jerusalem" and the surrounding nations are among the most volatile, violent, and dangerous places on earth.

Then what has happened to Isaiah's vision, and to Jesus' claim? Were they mere pie in the sky? Perhaps there is a clue in the final sentence of those words of Isaiah which we have heard to-day: "O House of Jacob, come, let us walk in the light of the Lord".

"Walk" is the instruction. "Come, let us go" he had imagined the nations saying earlier in the piece. We are on our way, we are making a journey, and we are on pilgrimage. The Kingdom of God is always a work in progress, and will continue to be so until the end of time. The first coming of Jesus in our human nature marked its beginning: only with His second coming at the end of time will it be complete.

In the interim, we have to walk, and we have to work. We have to work at building the Kingdom, at being peacemakers, at establishing justice; and we have to begin at home, in our own hearts, in our own lives, in our own families, and workplaces, and dealings with others; and from there we have to spread our work of being peacemakers into every place that we go, every situation in which we find ourselves.

We have to work, and we have to walk. The Second Vatican Council spoke of the Church as the Pilgrim People of God. A pilgrim people is a people on a journey, not a people which has already arrived. Like the nations of Isaiah's vision, making their way towards the Jerusalem Temple, we, both as individuals and as the Church, are making our way towards the Kingdom, this Kingdom whose presence has begun, and which we are helping to build, even as we travel towards it.

Journeys don't always go smoothly. There may be setbacks on the way: we may take wrong turnings: we may flounder at times; but we keep on travelling, correcting our mistakes, heading back to the correct route, keeping our goal always in mind and in sight.

And in our walking, on our pilgrimage, we have to be awake and alert. Sleepwalking is definitely not part of the agenda. St. Paul stresses that, as he calls on us to wake up. "Our salvation," he says "is even nearer than when we were converted". We are further along our pilgrim way: the final coming of the Kingdom is closer than it was.

Our Lord makes the same point in the Gospel. "Stay awake" He orders us, and "Stand ready" because He is coming. Yes He is coming at the end of time: He is coming too at the moment of our own death. But just as importantly, He is coming at every moment of our lives. He is coming in all the opportunities He offers us for building the Kingdom by acting as peacemakers, by doing His will. He is coming in our moments of prayer, when we are still and silent before Him, even though we may not be immediately conscious of His presence.

He is coming in the people whom we encounter, in whom we serve or reject HIM. He is coming in the moments of sorrow and failure, when He invites us to share with Him in the Garden of the Agony and in the abandonment of the Cross. He is coming in the moments of joy, when he allows us a foretaste of the Resurrection. He is coming in the gathering of His people to celebrate His death and resurrection in the Eucharist: in His word, spoken to us in the Scriptures; and in the sacrament and sacrifice of His Body and Blood.

If we are not awake we shall fail to recognise Him, as the world failed to recognise His first coming; and opportunities of building the Kingdom, of advancing along our pilgrim way, will be lost. Wake up, walk, and work. And be alert. Advent tells us that Christ is coming: not simply that He HAS come, in the past, in the Bethlehem stable, or even that He WILL come, in the future, on the clouds of heaven, but most importantly that He DOES come, here and now, in every moment of our lives. Are we awake to receive Him? If WE are not, there is no hope for the nations.

Reflection 2 Is.11:1-10, Ps.71:1-2,7-8,12-13,17, Rom.15:4-9, Matt.3:1-12

Wackiness for the Kingdom

If Isaiah's prophecy in that first reflection struck you as a tad optimistic—nations turning swords into ploughshares, universal peace arriving—today's may seem stark raving barmy. It is hard to imagine lions turning vegetarian or child-friendly cobras.

We have to remember that it is a vision, a dream if you like, and God help us if we ever give up on our dreams. Isaiah has a vision of universal harmony, no longer just among human beings, but among the whole of creation.

Like the previous vision, it is a prophecy of the Kingdom of God, but of that Kingdom fully realised, fully established. As we know, we are a long way from that situation, yet as we have also heard, the Kingdom of God has begun; it has arrived with the First Coming of the Messiah, the Christ, though it will be complete only with His Second Coming: it is a work in progress.

And it may be fair to say that, particularly over the past half century, the work towards that aspect of the Kingdom has advanced considerably. People have become aware of the inter-dependence of creation; that human beings, animals, plants, seas, trees, rivers, soil, depend upon one another: that we cannot continue plundering the earth as we have done in the past, without dire consequences.

Very often, the people behind this realisation, those who are encouraging us to "go green", may not be aware that what they are doing is to advance the Kingdom of God, to move us closer to the fulfilment of Isaiah's vision, yet that is what they are doing. Pope Benedict XVI was particularly conscious of this, and he worked hard to make the Church more environmentally aware, more clear that God's Kingdom cannot be divorced from God's creation, that human beings have stewardship of the earth, and that this entails a careful, even reverent, responsibility for it, a responsibility which will bring Isaiah's vision closer to reality.

Some aspects of the environmental movement may seem and may indeed be, wacky and way out: some environmental schemes actually do harm, rather than good, but this serves to remind us that creation shares humankind's fallen condition; that until the Kingdom of God is fully established, nothing is perfect, nothing is unambiguous.

Furthermore, Christians should be the last people to be deterred by an appearance of wackiness. Our Lord Himself appeared way out to the people of His generation, which was one reason why they crucified Him. Until the Emperor Constantine made

Christianity respectable, the followers of Christ were regarded as wacky: that was why they were persecuted. Our own English martyrs, like all the martyrs of every land and time, disturbed the Establishment by being out of the rut—and they paid with their lives.

Today we encounter John the Baptist—and if you want "wacky" you need look no further than him. A vegetarian (or even a vegan) he lived on locusts and wild honey. An apparent hippy, he wore a garment of camel hair. A disruptive element, he called the religious establishment "a brood of vipers"; and like so many before and after him, he was persecuted and finally executed for his outspokenness.

But notice one thing: this outspokenness, this difference, this being out of the rut, was never mere exhibitionism or self-advertisement. He was always concerned to point away from himself to the one who was to come after him: his focus was always on the Kingdom of God, and his whole mission, his whole life's enterprise, was summed up in one word: "prepare".

John the Baptist's mission was to prepare the way for the one who was to follow him, Jesus the Christ. Our mission, strange (indeed wacky) though it may seem, is to do the same: to prepare the way for the Second Coming of the Christ by helping to build the Kingdom of God.

In doing this, our present Holy Father has encouraged us not to worry about appearing wacky, or out of step. A year or so ago, the leadership group of women religious in America had their knuckles rapped by the Congregation of the Doctrine of the Faith, which used to be called the Holy Office. Shortly after settling into the See of Peter, Pope Francis told these women to remain courageous, and if they do receive a rebuke from the CDF, not to be too concerned about it. They are not to go seeking attention on their own behalf, but they are to be more concerned about preparing a way for the Lord, about building the Kingdom of God, than about keeping the authorities happy.

Apparently, Francis is upsetting some right wing groups, especially in America, by focusing more on Christ and on His Kingdom than on rules and regulations. Like John the Baptist before him, and indeed like Our Lord, he is prepared to appear wacky and out of step. No doubt, as with John the Baptist, and with Our Lord, there will be those, even within the Church, who will seek to bring him down.

We need to hear Pope Francis' call to be courageous in building the Kingdom; and we need to remember, with his predecessor Pope Benedict, that this involves, among other things, care for God's creation.

Reflection 3   **Is.35:1-6,10, Ps.14:6-10, Jam.5:7-10,**
                                                                                           Matt.11:2-11

Patience with the provisional

Today's Gospel is both disturbing and encouraging. Put yourself in John the Baptist's place for a moment. He has been so sure of his mission, and so confident in Jesus as the Messiah. He has spoken of Him as the one who is going to turn the world upside down, separating the wheat from the chaff, and giving the wicked their come-uppance. He has pointed Him out to his own disciples as the Lamb of God, and has allowed those disciples to leave him in order to follow the Lamb. His faith and his confidence have been total.

Yet now here he is, languishing in prison, facing execution and nothing is happening. The wicked are still in control, the world goes on much as it always did, and the supposed Messiah either cannot or doesn't wish to do anything to help His forerunner, His herald.

And so seeds of doubt are planted in the Baptist's mind. "Have I been getting it wrong? Is this not the Messiah after all? Has my whole life been built on an illusion?" And in the message which he sends, we can detect a note of frustration, even of anger: "ARE you the one who is to come?" the implication being "because, if you are, it is time you got your finger out".

It is disturbing to find someone's faith teetering, to observe the foundations of their life on the verge of collapse. And yet it is encouraging too, to know that even the greatest of men (and that is how Our Lord describes John the Baptist) have their moments of uncertainty, of anguish, of fear.

We may perhaps envy those who seem to drift, or even charge, their way through life untroubled, while we struggle with uncertainties, failures, and setbacks. The Baptist's experience shows us that we are not alone in our puzzlement, our fear, our desire sometimes to throw in the towel. Even the greatest, even the holiest, even the most dedicated of men and women may wake up on cold and dark moments and ask themselves "Have I got it wrong?"

There is encouragement in that, but there is encouragement too in Our Lord's answer, which seems only half an answer until we examine it more closely. Jesus doesn't say outright "Yes I am. Stop fretting. Everything in the garden is wonderful. Smile—God loves you" as those ghastly smiley badges used to proclaim a few years ago.

Instead His reply is "Look and think a bit more deeply. Don't demand simple answers which call for nothing from you—not faith, not struggle, not self-sacrifice. See the signs of the Kingdom, and follow where they lead you."

The signs to which Jesus points are those which Isaiah had prophesied as the indicators of the Kingdom of God: "the eyes of the blind shall be opened, the ears of the deaf unsealed, the lame shall leap like the deer, and the tongues of the dumb sing for joy". Our Lord points out that He is doing these and adds a few more for good measure.

Yet, not all the blind see: not all the lame walk, and so on. The Kingdom is here, but its fullness is not yet. The Messiah, the bringer of the Kingdom, is going to suffer, and His forerunner, His herald, His prophet, will have to suffer too. John must learn to be patient in his prison.

Karl Rahner, the great 20th century German Jesuit theologian, entitled his commentary on this passage "Patience with the provisional" (in "Everyday Faith".) In this life, there is a sense in which everything is provisional: we are not going to see the Kingdom in all its glory. Not all our questions are going to be answered at a stroke: not all our difficulties resolved. Mary Poppins is not going to come floating down under her umbrella to put everything to rights.

Like John the Baptist, we need to have patience with the provisional; and that means, among other things, patience with ourselves, with our own weaknesses, limitations and shortcomings. It is no accident that the second reading chosen for today is a call to patience. As in the days of Isaiah, as in the prison cell of John the Baptist, so people in the aftermath of the Lord's Resurrection and Ascension were eager for instant results: "What do we want?" "The return of the Messiah." "When do we want it?" "Now!"

"Sorry," says St. James, "life isn't like that. God's time is not our time." Or, as St. Peter put it, "With God, a day can mean a thousand years, and a thousand years the same as a day." But patience is not the same as doing nothing, as twiddling our thumbs.

Like the Baptist, we need to take heed of what we hear and see. The signs of the Kingdom are all around us: sickness is healed; there are great advances in medical and other sciences; a desire for peace and justice grows, even if its growth is uneven; the Good News is preached to the poor; and the living God is given to us as Eucharistic food. We have need for patience: we have no need for pessimism. Jesus the Christ is the one who was to come. He has come, and He is among us. Let us rejoice in the presence of His Kingdom: let us not be downhearted because its glory is not yet.

Reflection 4   **Is.7:10-14, Ps.23:1-6, Rom.1:1-7, Matt.1:18-24**

The unsung hero

A couple of years ago—or maybe even last year—I was given a CD of Flanders and Swann. For the benefit of anyone under the age of fifty, I should explain that Flanders and Swann were a pair of rather aristocratic musical comedians who performed wearing dinner suits. Michael Flanders, a large bearded man, was confined to a wheelchair, whilst Donald Swann, a balding, apparently rather nervous type, played the piano. Their repertoire contained such gems as The Hippopotamus Song, The Gasman Cometh, and I'm a Gnu.

Forty years ago, I thought they were hilarious. I listened with eager anticipation to this CD, and thought "Oh. All right. Was that it?" Like much of the humour of its day, it hadn't lasted well. What once seemed amusing was now flat, or even irritating.

I mention them, as I have done before, because one of their songs concerned the Unsung Heroes of the World. I am sure that the greatest unsung hero, though Flanders and Swann don't mention him, was St. Joseph.

We adore Jesus, the Son of God; we honour Mary, the Mother of God; Joseph we sort of notice in passing. Yet without Joseph, the whole story of redemption would have been very different. It would still have taken place—Joseph isn't absolutely essential to the Incarnation—but it would have been forced to take a very different route.

If Joseph had made a song and dance about Mary's pregnancy, if he had refused to take her as his wife, if he had declined to take responsibility for the upbringing of this child, who was to become known as "the son of the carpenter" we should have been faced with a history far removed from that with which we are familiar.

Joseph does not have an easy time of it. He is not imprisoned and beheaded like John the Baptist, he is not crucified like the one who was brought up as his son, and he does not have to stand at the foot of the Cross like Mary his wife. Instead, he is harried from pillar to post, constantly ordered around by heavenly messengers—"take Mary as your wife....take the Child and His Mother"—baffled and confused by this mysterious Child: "Did you not know that I must be about my Father's business?". Denied normal marital relations, he is nevertheless required to spend himself utterly, meeting the needs of a growing child, while coming to terms with the earth-shattering reality that this is the Messiah, the Son of God.

He is able to do it because he is a "just" man. The translation sometimes given—a man of honour—misses the point. Joseph is dikaios, just, because like Abraham his forebear, he has faith which justifies. He trusts in God, and thus becomes righteous, just, in the sight of God. And it is this justifying faith which carries him through the trials which surround the birth and infancy of the Son of God.

There is a sense in which Joseph is Everyman. Don't we all spend much of our time trying to make sense of life, and in particular trying to fathom the ways of God? Doesn't life for most of us take unexpected turns, throw up unlooked for challenges? Don't our relationships puzzle and confuse us from time to time, requiring of us that we press on in faith, trust, and hope? And isn't it the case that, if we have a strong faith in God, we have to rely on that faith at times to carry us through, as we flounder in the dark, unable to grasp God's purposes, but being compelled to trust that God does indeed have a purpose for us, and that our faith will prove to be justified, and to justify us, to make us, like St. Joseph, men and women who are just?

And when I say that Joseph is Everyman, perhaps I can be gender specific, and say that he is every MAN, because there is something particularly masculine about his puzzlement, his being out of the loop, his hovering helplessly in the background, while Mary gets on with the practicalities.

If the summons of the last reflection's readings was to patience, the call this week is to faith—faith in the sense of trust in God at times when life is confusing, when we are faced with situations beyond the normal run, when we are called to deal with what may seem beyond our strength. Faith is the call, and Joseph, the just man, is the model.

Reflection 5   Is.9:1-7, Ps.95:1-3,11-13, Titus 2:11-14

Journey into danger

I was surprised on Sunday by the number of people who told me they were going away for Christmas—I don't think it was anything personal. Later, as I listened to the weather reports, I felt compelled to offer a silent prayer for their safety, and to think "Sooner them than me".

Journeys can be enjoyable experiences, but often there is more misery than joy: inconvenience, discomfort, even danger can accompany those who are forced to travel. The journey taken by Joseph and Mary from Nazareth to Bethlehem was hardly a joy ride, and their experience at journey's end of finding the inns full and of having to make do with the manger in the stable can only have piled further stress and anxiety onto an already fraught situation.

Yet in the joy of the Saviour's birth, so much of the misery and even of the ongoing inconvenience will have been forgotten. Mary's pain and Joseph's worry will have dissolved into joy and awe at the birth of a child who is more than a child: a Saviour, a Messiah, the Son of God.

Even the absence of family and friends was compensated for by the arrival of a wider world: shepherds and wise men, and a whole cosmic dimension of heavenly beings, all foreshadowing the worshippers who were to travel, from that day onwards, to adore the Saviour in cribs large and small, magnificent and humble, in every corner of the earth and the heavens.

Some of you will remember Christmas 1968, when the first human beings to travel behind the moon broadcast their own message of worship, as the Apollo astronauts read from the opening chapter of the Book of Genesis, beaming their paean of praise to a listening world.

Journeys have always been part of the human experience, and will continue to be so until the end of time. We are told that our ancestors travelled out of Africa, a scientific confirmation of the Bible's pictorial description of our first parents' expulsion from the Garden of Eden, and of Cain's penalty of becoming a wanderer on the earth.

Jesus' more particular ancestors journeyed to the Promised Land from slavery in Egypt, and centuries later endured exile to, and return from , Babylon, part of modern day Iraq. Our Lord's own journey to Bethlehem in His mother's womb was the prelude to the family's flight into Egypt, and foreshadowed His final journey to death and resurrection in Jerusalem.

Like the Holy Family, every single one of us is on a journey, not only our personal trek from the cradle to the grave, but the pilgrimage of the People of God, the Church, to the fullness of the Kingdom. And like the journey from Nazareth to Bethlehem, our own life's journeys have their share of difficulty, disappointment, and danger.

This year, as every Christmas, there are countless people in the world whose journeys are far more perilous than our own, as people flee from fighting in Syria, Egypt, Nigeria, South Sudan, and many parts of the globe. Many of these people, who go in terror of their lives, are targeted purely because they are Christians, people who recognise and serve that child born in a stable to redeem the whole of humankind. Again it seems that history repeats itself over and over again, as the murderous wrath which King Herod directed against the infants of Bethlehem has its modern counterpart in the targeting of Christians today.

Tonight, as part of our life's pilgrimage, we have made our annual journey to the crib. We have come once again to recall that much earlier journey, not only from Nazareth to Bethlehem, but from heaven to earth. We have come to add our worship to that of the angels and the shepherds, and of the countless millions who have followed them down through the centuries.

As we do so, may we feel all the wonder, joy, and awe of this feast; but let us remember all those people, in many parts of the world, whose Christmas journeys may be fraught with danger, or who are suffering in refugee camps or bomb-shattered homes. May the Prince of Peace, who was born at Bethlehem, shed His peace on our troubled world, and may He turn us into peacemakers for the sake of that world.

Reflection 6

Is.42:1-4,6-7, Ps.28:1-4,9-10, Acts 10:34-38, Matt.3:13-17

YOU are the Beloved

We have come a long way in a short time. Only last week we were with the wise men worshipping at the stable, and now here we are at the River Jordan as the adult Jesus is baptised and begins His mission. Thirty years have passed in seven days.

Yet in another sense, no time at all has passed. We are still celebrating the Epiphany, the showing forth of the Son of God. Whereas now we tend to associate Epiphany only with the visit of the Magi, the showing-forth of Jesus to the non-Jewish nations, in the early Church the main focus of Epiphany was that which we celebrate today, the showing forth of Jesus as the Beloved Son of the Father, the Second Person of the Trinity.

Also in the early Church, as I have mentioned before, the Epiphany had a third part, the showing forth of the Lord's glory as He performed His first miracle, or sign, by turning water into wine at the marriage feast of Cana. One year in every three, that event is recalled in the Gospel for the Second Sunday in Ordinary Time, but this is not one of those years.

So it seems from the Church's history that the main emphasis today should be on the "showing forth" of Jesus, as the Father's voice speaks and proclaims Him as the Beloved Son of the Father, on whom the Father's favour rests. It is the next part of the jigsaw which is the Christmas season. The first part, the birth of the Messiah, showed Him to the Jewish people in the persons of Mary, Joseph, and the shepherds as their long awaited Saviour. Then the visit of the wise men, representing the pagan nations, showed Him to the whole world. Now He is shown as the Beloved Son of the Father, and the Cana miracle will show Him as the one who possesses glory, the attribute of God Himself.

This feast, then, like the rest of the season, calls us to focus on the person of Jesus, to root our lives in Him. Has it any other implications for us?

Listen again to the words of the Father, spoken from heaven, spoken as Jesus emerges from His Baptism: "This is my Son, the Beloved, my favour rests on Him." Like Jesus, you have been baptised. As with Jesus, so when you were baptised, the Holy Spirit descended on you. And the Father has said, and continues to say, about you: "This is my son/daughter the Beloved. My favour rests on him/her."

The Lord's Baptism focuses our attention on Him, but there is a sense in which it focuses also on us as people who, like Him, and in Him, have been baptised, and therefore are beloved children of the Father, people on whom God's favour rests; people of immense worth, and value, and dignity, who should therefore never undervalue ourselves.

That is the plus side of our own association with this feast, namely the dignity and worth which it bestows upon us. But there is a price to pay, which we recognise when we listen to the voice of the prophet, speaking of God's Beloved, of His Chosen One on whom His favour rests.

Hear what the Lord has to say about His chosen, His child, His Beloved: "He does not break the crushed reed, nor quench the wavering flame." What does this mean? He doesn't put people down, make life more difficult for them, kick them when they are down, destroy such enthusiasm or self-respect as they have. What about us? Do we do that? Pope Francis is concerned, perhaps rightly, that the Church has too often done that, has borne down harshly on people, has focused too much on rules and prohibitions, instead of supporting their weakness, sheltering the stuttering flame until it was ready to flare out. In particular, he wants the confessional to be, as it was intended, a meeting place with the compassionate Christ.

Harshness is what we are called to avoid. But there are also positive things which, as the beloved sons and daughters of the Father, we are called to do.

"To bring true justice" is mentioned twice, along with an insistence that we persevere until "true justice is established on earth". There is a great deal of injustice on the earth—people wrongly imprisoned, priests barred on spurious grounds from exercising their priesthood, people in various parts of the world denied basic human rights, including, for many of the unborn, the right to life itself. As the beloved of the Father, the demand is made of us, not only that we act justly ourselves, but that we campaign and work for justice.

And there is more: "to open the eyes of the blind, to free captives from prison, and those who live in darkness from the dungeon." That ties in with working for justice, but it also calls on us to free people's minds and spirits, to show them how liberating the Gospel is when heard rightly, to show them the true face of Jesus Christ who offers liberty and life.

Today, both as individuals and as the Church, let us hear the Father's voice saying about us "This is my son/daughter, the beloved, my favour rest on him/her," and let us resolve to live out the full consequences of those words.

Reflection 7   Is.49:3,5-6, Ps.39:2,4,7-10, 1 Cor.1:1-3, Jn.1:29-34

The servant who takes away sin

In the previous reflection, I mentioned that the Feast of Epiphany originally had three parts: the visit of the wise men and the showing forth of Christ to the pagan nations, the Baptism—the showing forth of Our Lord as Son of God; and the marriage feast at Cana—the showing forth of His glory. I also mentioned that, one year out of three, the Marriage at Cana crops up as the Gospel for the Second Sunday in Ordinary Time, but that this isn't one of those years.

All of this is true and yet today's Gospel still has an "Epiphany" quality to it, as John the Baptist shows forth Our Lord as the Lamb of God. Indeed, when John talks about "revealing Him to Israel", the verb which he uses is, in Greek, "phaino", which has the same root as Epiphany.

So we are still in the business of Our Lord being "shown forth", this time as "the Lamb of God which takes away the sin of the world". Does that ring any bells? Of course it does. Every single day before Holy Communion Jesus is shown forth in exactly those words. Incidentally, when the new translation was introduced couple of years ago, the powers-that-be got their nether garments in a twist insisting that "sin" was an unacceptable translation, and that we had to say "sins" to translate the Latin plural "peccata", yet John the Baptist here says "sin" (singular). But then again, even John the Baptist wouldn't dare disagree with Italian monsignori.

Either way, it is as the Lamb of God that Jesus is shown forth, both by John the Baptist and in the Eucharist, as taking sin(s) away. Why is that? Scholars point to two things. Firstly, Jesus is the true Paschal lamb, the lamb that was slain at Passover, and whose blood protected the people of Israel from the Destroying Angel. Clearly that fits: Jesus was slain around the Feast of Passover, and gave His Body and Blood as food and drink at the time that the Paschal Lamb was eaten.

Secondly, John the Baptist may have in mind the Suffering Servant described by the prophet whom we call Second Isaiah, a servant described by the prophet as "like a lamb that is led to the slaughter" and which "bears the sins of many".

As the Lamb of God, Our Lord combines both these concepts from the Hebrew scriptures, concepts which bear fruit in His death on the Cross, and in the presence of that death sacramentally in the Eucharist.

Now if you or I had been responsible for putting together the Lectionary, we should probably have used that particular Servant Song from Second Isaiah as the First Reading today. Instead, to keep us on our toes, the actual compilers of the Lectionary have used a different Servant Song from the same prophet.

If you look at the beginning of that reading, you will see that the prophet addresses the servant as "Israel". In other words there is a sense in which the whole people are God's servant. Then, though, he goes on to speak to the servant as an individual, who is going to bring back the people of Israel, and indeed of all the nations, to God. So the whole people are called to be God's servants, but there is also an individual who will represent the nation, and we can see that individual as being Jesus, Our Lord.

What is that servant to do? He is to bring the people of Israel back to God, which recalls Jesus' birth as the Jewish Messiah, but He is also to be the light of the nations, which takes us back to the visit of the wise men, representing the non-Jewish nations.

Are you still with me? If so, you are probably worn out, but we still have to ask the weekly question "What does this mean for us?" Well, there is a call to be alert, to recognise, with John's disciples, Jesus as the Lamb of God who takes away the sin(s) of the world, when He is held up before us, and given to us as food, in Holy Communion. There is a call, too, to be constantly deepening our understanding of the Eucharist, to recognise the richness, and awesomeness, and power of this sacrament. We need to recognise too that we, like John the Baptist's followers, are called to be disciples of Jesus following Him, spending time with Him, allowing His life to grow within us.

Finally we are reminded that we too, in Jesus, are servants of the Lord, called to live and give our lives to and with Him. If we can grasp some of this the potential for growth is there in us.

Reflection 8   Is.8:23-9:3, Ps.26:1,4,13-14, 1 Cor.1:10-13,17, Matt.4:12-23

Get a move on!

Sometimes it may strike you that you need to get a move on. Most of the time, life muddles along, each day much the same as the one before, but every so often you know that the time has come when you must shift up a gear or three. You know that NOW you have to think about getting married, or following a call to the priesthood or religious life, or changing your job, or emigrating, or whatever. Perhaps you can't say exactly why you know that the time has come for action, but you feel strongly that it has.

If you are like me, you may be a bit reluctant to act. It can be easier to carry on in the same old way, putting off decisions, delaying action. My father, God rest his good soul, saw his 65th birthday come and go, his old age pension kick in, and yet he would have carried on indefinitely, getting up at half past six every morning, working in the shop till 7:30 every night, had my mother not suffered a burst ulcer, thus confronting him with the uncomfortable truth that this was no longer a wise lifestyle for either of them, and that they needed to look for a new house, sell up, and retire.

I might never have seriously considered a vocation to priesthood, had I not, for some unknown reason, acquired the habit of dropping in to the Cathedral to visit the Blessed Sacrament on my way back to work at the end of my dinner hour.

Yet, once these things happen, you know that you have to act upon them, that you have no business to put them off. We see that scenario being acted out in today's Gospel, both for Our Lord, and for His first disciples.

For Jesus, it appears to be news of the arrest of John the Baptist which stirs Him to action. This is the trigger both for His move to Galilee and for His conviction that He is now called to fulfil Isaiah's prophecy of the light which is to shine upon Zebulun and Naphtali.

It is also the moment for Him to begin His mission, a mission which will lead inexorably to the Cross, a mission which will change the whole of history. "From that moment" we are told "Jesus began His preaching" His proclamation of the Kingdom or reign of God which was the driving force of His remaining years on earth. Matthew's use of the phrase "from that moment" is echoed in St. Mark, who repeatedly uses the word "immediately" ("at once").

Nor is it only for Our Lord Himself that the moment for decisive action has come. Jesus has already begun to recruit disciples—we heard in John's Gospel how the Baptist pointed his own followers in Jesus' direction with the words "Behold the Lamb of God" and how those first disciples spent time with Him before drawing others to Him in their turn—and now He calls these disciples to action.

They like us have been getting along with life, pursuing their daily occupation as fishermen, but now it is time for them to put their discipleship into action. I mentioned that St. Mark several times applies the expression "at once" to Our Lord's behaviour at this stage: now St. Matthew applies the same expression twice to the fishermen-disciples.

Both pairs of brothers—Simon and Andrew, James and John—are busy with their daily affairs: both are called: both respond "at once". From the time that John the Baptist pointed them in Jesus' direction they may have been pondering their future: now the time for pondering is replaced by the time for action.

What about us? What is our time for action? What is our time for responding to the call of the Lord? Almost certainly, it is today. It may not be a call to a life-changing decision. Perhaps it is a call to be less selfish, to be more considerate within the family. Perhaps it is a call to write that letter, send that email, and make that phone call that you have been putting off. Perhaps a call to visit that person, who, you feel, may be in need of a friendly word, a bit of company.

On the other hand, perhaps you are being called to shed a bad habit, to take a more positive attitude, to engage with life a little more fully: or perhaps to make a real effort to deepen your prayer life. Whatever it may be, the time to do it is "at once"; and if you do it, you will be playing your own part in fulfilling Jesus' mission of proclaiming the Kingdom of God, and helping to build that Kingdom.

Reflection 9 — Mal.3:1-4, Ps.23:7-10, Heb.2:14-18, Luke 2:22-40

Light for a darkened world

It is probably fair to say that the Church has, in effect, three festivals of light. Christmas, replacing the Roman celebration of Sol Invictus, the Unconquered Sun, marks the birth of the Christ, the light of the world: Easter, the great feast, recalls with the kindling of the Easter fire and the holding aloft of the Paschal candle, the final triumph of that light over evil, sin, and death: and now, between the two, we have this almost disregarded feast of Candlemas, the Presentation of the Lord, when we recall that the Light of the World was hailed as such by Simeon at the entry into the Temple.

This feast takes place when it does because the Presentation, the event which it describes, happened forty days after the Saviour's birth, but I suspect that our emphasis on the "light of the nations" aspect of it, with the blessing and lighting of candles, has been influenced, like the fixing of the date of Christmas, by the desire to remind us again of light in winter, of the light shining in darkness, a darkness which is not only the metaphorical darkness of sin and evil, but the very real physical darkness which covers so much of the earth at this time of year.

We are all ready for some light, are we not? It hasn't been a cold winter, but it has been a wretched winter; grey, overcast, wet, submerging large parts of the country under floodwater, hiding the sun from all of us. We all need to see the sun, to feel its healing warmth, to be encouraged by real daylight. The blessing and lighting of candles today helps us to look forward to the lighting of the Great Candle at Easter, but it is also a reminder, in more worldly terms, that winter won't last forever—that earthly light, as well as the light of Christ, is on its way back.

But what OF the light of Christ, whom Simeon hailed as "a light to enlighten the pagans"? Does the world need that this year, at this time of year?

Surely only a fool would deny that we do. We like to believe that our world is becoming more civilised, and in some respects it is, yet almost unbelievable acts of barbarity continue. The horror stories emerging from Syria, of tortures almost beyond imagining, of chemical attacks, and of mass murder, are somehow even more horrendous because they are the work of a government headed by a suave, sophisticated, London-trained ophthalmic surgeon, who was regarded originally as the great hope of a nation already scarred by his brutal father. The suicide bombings, murder, and destruction in many parts of that region and beyond, are the more sickening as being carried out by people who claim to believe in God under the title "the compassionate, the merciful".

In our own country, not a day goes by without reports of murders, assaults, abuse, cyber-bullying, or neglect, while the mass murder entailed in abortion is presented as a human right. Meanwhile, across the Atlantic, the United States has 30,000 deaths by firearms every year, 18,000 of which are self-inflicted; whilst to the south, in Mexico, drug related gang murders are a daily occurrence.

Do the nations need their light? Assuredly they do. Here in the Northern hemisphere we need the light of the sun, but in common with the rest of the world we need that greater light, the child who is God, who entered His sanctuary on this day, and who was hailed as " a light to enlighten the Gentiles, and the glory of His people Israel".

Reflection 10   Eccl.15:15-20, 1 Cor.2:6-10, Matt.5:17-37

Love rules, but don't love rules

It is sometimes said that the Catholic Church is obsessed with sin, and you probably know the old story of the parish priest who was having his leaving "do" at which the Chairman of the Parish Council stood up and said "Ee, Father, we didn't know what sin was till you came to the parish".

Nonetheless, sin exists, and we can't ignore it. People will sometimes claim that the Old Testament was a mass of rules and regulations—and that the Church today has become the same—whereas Jesus swept all that away, and said, in effect, like an early Lennon and McCartney, "All you need is love".

There is an element of truth in that, but a far bigger element of caricature and misunderstanding. Much of it has to do with what Our Lord meant by "love". Remember His words "Greater love has no one than to lay down one's life for one's friends": remember His actions, living out those words to the full by going to the Cross.

Love is not an easier option than keeping rules: it is not another way of saying "Do what you like". In fact, keeping the rules can be far easier than practising genuine love, because we can stay detached, we needn't commit ourselves; whereas love demands involvement, self-giving, putting our hearts at risk. Not for nothing did the old song say "Love hurts".

All the examples which Our Lord gives in today's Gospel underline the far harder demands which true discipleship, true love, make upon us. Most of us are likely to succeed in avoiding killing people. "That is not enough," says Jesus: "you must avoid all the bitterness, contempt, name-calling which fall way short of actual murder." And when He adds that coming to worship God is a non-starter until we have sorted out our resentments and paid our debts of justice, then we really are called to some serious spiritual housekeeping.

Of course, the reaction of most of the world is to say "Well, it is hypocrisy to go to church if you are full of bitterness, so we won't go to church," which misses the point completely. The demand which Jesus makes of us is that we sort out our attitudes and relationships, AND THEN come to church: His call is definitely a matter of BOTH/AND.

Turning to sexual sin, again Jesus tightens, rather than loosens, the demands of the Law of Moses. His insistence here is that we do not regard people as sex objects, but that we respect them—and ourselves—as complete human beings. The legalistic approach which we can so easily adopt was caricatured a few years ago by David Lodge, in his novel "How far can you go?" pointing up an attitude with which we may be familiar—what can we get away with before it becomes a sin? This is the very attitude which Our Lord calls us to reverse. He demands that we view things positively: what behaviour, what thoughts are compatible with genuine love and respect?

I suppose that, for me, the difference between the two approaches was summed up by my Grammar School days. The school had a rule book, with which everyone was issued, entitled "Standing Orders", telling you where you couldn't ride your bike, where you couldn't go in town, probably when you couldn't blow your nose, and there was a whole army of prefects and members of staff—who were called masters, to remind us that we were serfs—trying to catch you out breaking rules that you didn't even know existed.

The consequence was that we learned to play the game, to keep just within the rules, to tug the forelock, to put on an innocent expression with a "Who sir? Me sir?" as if we were playing "The Vicar's Hat" while we viewed the whole system, and ourselves for going along with it, with a hefty measure of disgust and contempt.

This attitude of just sticking to the rules, and the sort of system which encourages it, is criticised by Our Lord as shallow virtue, the un-deep virtue of the scribes and Pharisees, and He warns that it won't get us to heaven. It is the attitude which one sometimes met when the rules stated that, to attend Mass, you had to be present for the Offertory, Consecration, and Priest's Communion, and there were people who would delay their arrival until just before the Offertory, and leave as soon as the priest had received communion.

I remember a certain parish where I was assistant priest 25 years ago. One Sunday evening, while the parish priest was saying Mass, I had to go out, but tried to make sure that I would be back in time to greet the people at the end of Mass. As I drove up to the church, I was taken aback to see people pouring out. "Heck" I thought, "Mass has finished early." Not a bit of it. It was communion time, and these people felt that they had ticked the box and could leave.

Is our attitude negative or positive? How deep does our virtue go? Are we content just to keep the rules, or are we prepared to listen when Jesus demands more from us?

Reflection 11

Lev.19:1-2, 17-18, Ps.102:1-4,8,10,12-13 1Cor.3:16-23, Matt.5:38-48

There's the rub

"What is REAL?" asked the Rabbit one day. "Does it mean having things that buzz inside you and a stick-out handle?"

"Real isn't how you are made" said the Skin Horse. "When a child loves you for a long, long time, not just to play with but REALLY loves you, then you become REAL."

"Does it hurt?" asked the Rabbit.

"Sometimes" said the Skin Horse. "When you are real, you don't mind being hurt."

"Does it happen all at once," he asked, "like being wound up?"

"It doesn't happen all at once," said the Skin Horse. "By the time you are real, most of your hair has been loved off, and you get very shabby: but once you are real, you can't become unreal again. It lasts for always." (Margery Williams: The Velveteen Rabbit)

"You must therefore be perfect, just as your heavenly Father is perfect" said Jesus, and we might imagine the Rabbit asking "What is PERFECT?" and receiving a reply in very similar terms.

"Perfect" is "perfectus", "thoroughly made": it is another word for "real" and it takes a lifetime, and it hurts, and it rubs most of your hair off, and it makes you shabby, and it probably leaves a whole trail of mistakes and mess in your wake, and it won't be complete when you die, which is what Purgatory is for, and it comes of being loved by God, who plays rough, and who chucks you about, and squeezes you tight.

"And does it really mean loving your enemies, like that teacher who made your life a misery, and the boss who picked on you at work, and that crotchety neighbour, and the pro-abortionists, and the jihadists, and the government, and the bishop, and Morecambe supporters?"

Yes, all of them, but like becoming real, it won't happen all at once. It will be a process, and it may be painful, and it will rub a bit more of your hair off, but it will be worth it in the long run, and it will even make you feel better, and it is all part of becoming "perfectus"—thoroughly made.

And don't forget that the Letter to the Hebrews, in the New Testament, says that even Jesus was made perfect—thoroughly made—through suffering.

"Yes—but Morecambe supporters!"

Well, some things will take a bit longer than others.

Reflection 12   Is.49:14-15, Ps.61:2-3,6-9, 1 Cor.4:1-5, Matt.6:24-34

Worried? Who's worried?

You may know the daft old story about the barmaid who goes down into the cellar to change a barrel. After half an hour, she hasn't reappeared, so the landlord goes down to check, and finds the barrel open, the beer all running away, and the barmaid sitting with her head in her hands, bawling her eyes out.

"Goodness me" says the landlord, as he would. "What has happened?" "Well," sobs the barmaid, "I started thinking. One day, I may get married, and I may have a daughter, and she may come to work here, and she may come down into the cellar, and someone may have spilt beer on the floor, and she may slip in the beer, and may fall, and bang her head, and die."

How much time and nervous energy do you and I waste worrying about things that may never happen, or which are totally beyond our control? If I am reading the newspaper, which I tend to do less and less often, I will come across things which annoy me, get me wound up, destroy my peace of mind, and I have to ask myself "Right. Is there anything I can do about this?"

Well, of course, the first answer to that is always "Yes" because I can pray about it: I can bring it to God. Do we do that? If things annoy or upset us, do we bring them to prayer? If not, why not? What does that say about our faith? about our relationship with God?

Is there anything else I can do? If there is, then I should do it: if not, then I should let it go. There is no point carrying it around with me, letting it destroy my peace of mind. That is the sort of useless anxiety against which Our Lord warns us. Far from making situations better, it makes them worse, because it makes us less able to deal with things; it upsets our equilibrium.

Some people, of course, are naturally anxious: they are born worriers. But if they can recognise that, realise that their anxieties are more a matter of temperament than of the actual situation, and if they can bring that situation to God and, as far as possible, leave it with Him, then life becomes more bearable.

On the other hand, Our Lord is not suggesting that we should float through life carelessly, without any concern for practical realities, like the grasshopper in Aesop's fable, who spends the summer idly chirruping away, unlike the ant who is storing up food for the winter. When winter comes, the ant is content: the grasshopper is in distress.

People do need to be concerned about the practicalities of life. There are people, not only in the developing world, but even in this country, who are asking, not "What are we to eat? What are we to wear?" but "Is there anything to eat? Have I any warm clothing?" These are not the frivolous or unnecessarily anxious questions against which Our Lord warns us: they are severely practical questions.

There should be no need in our world today for anyone to ask those questions. If people are going short, we have a duty to help them: we also have a duty to ask ourselves and the people in power how such a situation has arisen. At least since the late nineteenth century, Catholic Social Teaching has led the world in matters of justice, and Pope Francis, from his background of working in the slums, is anxious—no, I shouldn't say "anxious" should I?—is concerned that the Church today should maintain her focus on that teaching.

Answers posed by hunger, poverty, the unequal distribution of wealth, are not necessarily straightforward, but given the resources available to the nations of the world, they should be attainable. Our Lord calls us to set our hearts first on the Kingdom of God and on His righteousness: if governments were to do that, the world would undergo radical change.

And we, where do we set our hearts? And how fully do we realise the depth of God's love for us? "Does a mother forget her baby?" asks the prophet, answering that God's love for us is more intense than even that most powerful and fundamental of human loves. If only we could grasp that, how many of our anxieties would melt away, and how much freer would we be to work for justice?

Reflection 13 — Ex.17:3-7, Ps.94:1-2,6-9, Rom. 5:1-2,5-8, Jn.4:5-42

Water, water, everywhere

Water is one of the great themes of Lent and Easter. Throughout Lent, adults are being prepared for baptism at the Easter Vigil, and for those of us already baptised there will be, at the Vigil, the blessing of new water, the renewal of our baptismal vows, and the drenching with the Easter water.

In a climate like ours, it is easy to take water for granted. Indeed, for people in the south of England, it has often been the destructive, rather than the life-giving, power of water which struck home in a recent winter, and water was more of an enemy than a friend.

Yet even we are aware, often only subconsciously, that water is the stuff of life: without it we suffer and quickly die. For the peoples of the Middle East, that knowledge is an ever present reality.

Hence we can have a degree of sympathy with the Israelites who grumble when their journey across the wilderness finds them short of water. "Tormented by thirst" says the biblical writer, and if you have ever been slightly thirsty you may have some inkling of the real torment which lack of water can bring. The gift of water when Moses strikes the rock with his staff is literally the difference between life and a horrible death.

The woman of Samaria may not have been in such a critical condition, but the daily trek to the well with an empty bucket, and the journey back home with the extra weight when it was full, must have taken its toll on her strength and her patience.

Notice something else about this daily journey: she makes it "about the sixth hour", in other words at noon, when the sun would have been at its height, and no one (except mad dogs and Englishmen) would choose to make such a trip. Indeed, it is clear from her conversation with Our Lord that no one else is around.

Why should that be? What is she doing there, on her own, at the worst time of day? Clearly she is something of an outcast, with whom the other women of the town are not willing to associate. The reason for this emerges in the course of her conversation with Jesus, in that lovely exchange about her husband.

"I have no husband" says she, and Jesus quickly reveals that He knows her inside out. "Aye, you are right there: you've had five, and the one you have now isn't your husband." And the woman is too worldly wise to feel any shame at being found out, but instead retorts with rueful wit "I can see you are a prophet".

Someone who can go through blokes at that rate would clearly be perceived as a threat by the womenfolk. No wonder she was ostracised.

Yet Our Lord doesn't judge or condemn her. Instead He reveals to her His nature and identity as the Messiah. Have you thought how shocking that is? The Son of God reveals His identity to a woman (regarded at the time as inferior) to a Samaritan (a heretic from a group who had broken away from the Chosen People) to a serial monogamist or even adulteress. It is as if, in the 1960s, He had appeared to Christine Keeler or Mandy Rice-Davies, or today, given the rate at which she has been through husbands, to Joan Collins. The tabloids, and even the Church, would react with shock and horror. What we are to make of it I leave you to ponder.

Furthermore, it is to her that Our Lord reveals the concept of living water, which He would subsequently identify with the Holy Spirit, making this encounter a moment for expounding deep doctrine. And from there, the woman becomes a sort of apostle, spreading the Good News to the people of the town. I wonder if any of the women listened to her—if they did, she must really have spoken convincingly—or whether the Samaritans, whom the Gospel describes as "walking towards Him" were mainly men. Perhaps the women came along to keep an eye on their men folk.

So now we come to the weekly question: what is this saying to us? Firstly, given Our Lord's dealings with this somewhat way-out woman, there is a warning to us not to be judgmental. Also we are reminded that God can use whatever channels He wishes, however unusual or unorthodox, to spread the Gospel and to build the Kingdom. Thirdly, at a human level, we might learn to cherish the gift of water more than we tend to do, and to support charities such as Water Aid. Finally, at a supernatural level, we give thanks for our baptism, and ponder the presence of the Holy Spirit who dwells within us as water which is both living and life-giving.

Reflection 14   1 Sam.16:1,6-7,10-13, Ps.22, Eph.5:8-14, Jn.9:1-41

Do you see what I see?

You probably know the old saying "there are none so blind as those who will not see". That seems to be one of the principal messages of these readings.

It is certainly the message to the Pharisees. "You are not saying we are blind, are you?" they ask, and Our Lord replies "No. If you were blind, you would have an excuse for not seeing, but as you claim that you can see, you have no excuse."

Another problem, highlighted by the First Reading, is that we don't see correctly: we don't look in the right places. As Jesse's sons are brought to Samuel for inspection, God warns the prophet to stop judging by externals: "God does not see as man sees. Man looks at appearances, but God looks at the heart."

That can be a problem for all of us. We can too easily be taken in by appearances, especially today when salesmen, politicians (is there actually a difference between salesmen and politicians?)and all sorts of people in the public eye employ image consultants to burnish their appearance, to enhance their appeal. The expression "all fur coat and no knickers "comes to mind, but it isn't always easy to distinguish reality from show.

Then what about us? Are we authentic? Are we the real thing? The Church has taken a tremendous battering in recent years because of the amount of hypocrisy which has been uncovered, especially through the paedophile scandals, where people, mostly priests, who were supposed to be bringing Christ to others, have instead brought unspeakable horrors.

That is the extreme, but we know that all of us, to a greater or lesser degree, fall short of the ideal, which is forgivable provided we don't pretend to be living up to something which we are not. St. Francis of Assisi was once accosted by a man who said to him "Brother Francis, take care that you are always what people believe you to be" and I always pray with particular fervour, whenever it occurs in the Divine Office, that portion of the psalm which reads

"Let not those who hope in you be put to shame through me, Lord of hosts,

Let not those who seek you be dismayed through me, God of Israel"

and I am often disturbed by the thought that people may believe me to be something which I am not.

But what about our seeing? What do we fail, or even refuse, to see? I suspect that our blessings are things which we often overlook, often fail to recognise. Our loved ones, our health, running water, electricity, the ability to travel more or less where we wish, sufficient food, fresh air, freedom, the amount of sheer beauty in the world: how often do we notice these things? How often do we give thanks for them? I remember a barber many years ago—and bear in mind that barbers are often repositories of wisdom—saying "If I asked anyone who came in here, what are you really short of? they wouldn't be able to answer", and that, of course, is before we even begin to think of the love of God, the presence in our lives of Jesus Christ, the sacraments, especially the sacrament of His Body and Blood, our union in the Church with all those throughout the world and all those who have gone before us.

Then, what about our neighbour, both our immediate neighbours and those spread throughout the earth? When we see them, or think of them, do we see the face of Christ in them, however heavily it may be disguised, or do we see a potential enemy, a threat, a competitor? Do we see the needs of our worldwide brothers and sisters? Do we see the needs of those on our doorstep, whether it is the need of a loaf of bread, a kind word, or simply a few moments of our time?

When Jesus cured the blind man, He enabled him to see the world for the first time. Perhaps we need that same gift of sight, to see the world anew, to see it with the eyesight and the inner sight which Jesus has given us and, in seeing the world anew, to see Him with greater clarity as our Messiah and Lord.

Reflection 15   Ez.37:12-14, Ps.129, Rom.8:8-11, Jn.11:1-45

Dead or alive

Many many moons ago, in a previous parish, I was called to a deathbed. After the person died, I was leading prayers, while the family stood around the bed, and I read the passage from today's Gospel in which Our Lord speaks of Himself as the Resurrection and the Life.

"If anyone believes in me, even though they die, yet shall they live" I read, "and whoever lives and believes in me will never die." And as I read the words "Do you believe this?" the whole family shouted out "YES".

The raising of Lazarus is important, not so much as an event but as a sign. Lazarus would die again, but in raising him to life Jesus was pointing him to a life beyond earthly death, that death which is not final but which marks the flowering of eternal life. That is the sense in which it is true to say that believers in Jesus will never die. Our earthly life will come to an end, but that will mark our passage to a new stage in life, indeed to the fullness of life for which we were created.

This involves a different understanding of death, a different understanding of life. When God, speaking through Ezekiel, promises to open the peoples' graves, and to raise them from their graves, He is suggesting that currently they are dead, not because they have ceased to live and breathe, but because their exile in Babylon is a living death. By enabling them to return home from exile, God will be giving them new life.

Just as there are said to be more ways than one of killing a cat, so there are more ways than one of being dead, more ways than one of being alive. The early part of Charles Dickens' "A Tale of Two Cities" is entitled "Recalled to life", a title which plays out in two ways. Firstly, Dr. Manette, who has been a prisoner for so long in the Bastille that he has lost his mind, is set free and restored both to his family and, eventually, to health and sanity: then Charles Darnay, on trial for his life, is acquitted and freed from the shadow of the gallows. There are ways in which we can be dead while physically and mentally still alive, while the raising of Lazarus holds out the promise of life beyond earthly death.

St. Paul is making the same point to the Christians in Rome. When he speaks about our bodies being dead through sin, he is thinking not only of physical death, but of the lethargy, lifelessness, and captivity to earthly desires which he sees as the results of sin. Likewise, the life of Christ and His Spirit within us is a present reality, not simply something which will follow bodily death. Indeed, Paul scarcely takes note of the death of the body; the life and death of which he is speaking take place on both sides of the grave.

This ties in with Our Lord's teaching about eternal life, and about the Kingdom of God. Just as the Kingdom is already present, though its glory is not yet, so we already possess eternal life, though we still await its fullness.

There is a similar point to be recognised when Lazarus emerges from the tomb. Although he is alive, he is still not free. The "bands of stuff" which bind him, and the cloth around his face, symbolise all the messy things of life which prevent us from being fully alive. Even when Lazarus' physical life has been restored, there are aspects of death which cling to him, as sin which is closely allied to death clings to us, even as we try to live in Christ.

Some of you may be familiar with prayer of the imagination as practised by St. Ignatius Loyola, in which you imagine yourself in a scene from the Gospels, and immerse yourself in it. I have to confess that this rarely works for me, though some people find it immensely helpful. The raising of Lazarus is one of very few episodes in which I can manage this prayer of the imagination, and I would suggest it to you as something which you might try.

It entails imagining yourself as Lazarus, lying in the depth of the tomb, lifeless and also bound. You hear the voice of Jesus calling you by name, and saying "Come out". His voice courses through you, giving you life once more, enabling you to stagger towards the daylight, where you hear the voice of the Lord again saying "Unbind him/her. Let him/her go free." Then you feel all that binds you being stripped away—your bad habits, your repeated sins, your sluggishness, your bitterness, your lack of charity. You let go of all these things, allowing them to drop away, so that you stand free, in the light, fully alive. If you give yourself wholeheartedly to this exercise, it may become, no longer a matter of the imagination, but something which the Lord does for you in reality.

Reflection 16   Ex.12:1-8,11-14, Ps.115:12-13,15-18, 1Cor.11:23-26, Jn.13:1-15

A homily for Holy Thursday

I have a sneaking suspicion, though I may, of course, be wrong, that the people who are to have their feet washed tonight will have washed them already before coming to Mass. It isn't always so.

Very clearly etched on my mind is Holy Thursday 1988. I was based at the Diocesan Youth Centre at the time, where we were celebrating the Triduum with a group of young people from all over the Diocese. We were dramatising the Gospel, incorporating the foot-washing into the reading, with one of the young people speaking Peter's lines, while I both read and played the part of Jesus.

As I approached Peter, I saw that he had the dirtiest foot I have ever encountered in my life. Not only had he not washed it in preparation for Mass, it appeared not to have been washed all year. As he spoke Peter's lines very dramatically, I was overtaken by a massive attack of the giggles.

You know what it is like when you are smitten by the giggles in the most inappropriate setting? The harder you try to suppress them, the worse it becomes. As I looked down at the words I had to speak, I could see Becher's Brook looming: "No one who has taken a bath needs washing. He is clean all over." That was bad enough, but there was worse to come, "You too are clean—though not all of you are."

By this time, I was almost helpless with silent laughter. The priest who was following me with the towel had stuffed the corner of it into his mouth, so that he wouldn't burst out. I took a run at the words, failed, and tried again. In the end, they rushed out in a sort of falsetto scream, exactly like Brian Johnston's disaster on Test Match Special after Aggers' description of Ian Botham's dismissal. Meanwhile, the cause of the mirth remained blissfully unaware of the havoc he was creating.

I mention that incident partly because there was something appropriate about it. We are, or we should be, as the Church, the people of mucky feet. I said this years ago, preaching at the Cathedral, and now I find that Pope Francis has said virtually the same thing.

The Pope has said that he wants a Church which is stained and mucky through becoming involved in the messiness of people's lives, in the chaos of the world. (The Pope, in fact, agrees with me, so he must be right—I mean, I must be right.) If we are to be, as the Church, truly the Body of Christ, then we cannot float above the world, immune from its stresses and pains. This is not what Jesus the Christ did. He wandered among the sick and the broken-hearted, he associated with sinners, and the so-called good people were scandalised (as some people today are scandalised by the Pope). Jesus' feet were travel-stained from tramping among the poor of the Kingdom. He carried with Him the smell of the sheep, as Francis tells us to do.

Of course we know that the Church has become stained in a very bad way, through the paedophile scandals. For these stains we must beg forgiveness: they are the mark of the devil, not of Jesus Christ. Nonetheless, we must continue to be the people of mucky feet, tramping in the footsteps of Jesus Christ, walking confidently and lovingly among His erring sheep, following Him, if necessary, to the Cross.

GOOD FRIDAY: 2014 A HOMILY DELIVERED AT Ss. Mary and James, Scorton, where the Catholics of Scorton and Claughton were joined by parishioners from the Church of England and Methodist churches for the Solemn Commemoration of the Passion. The Anglicans and Methodists received Communion from the Vicar, while the Catholics received from the priest.

Christ's body hangs broken on the Cross. It is still broken today: we cannot share the Body of Christ, the Eucharist, with one another. Yet brokenness is not the whole story: the broken body rose from the tomb, still pierced, still wounded, yet glorious, and we too are called to rise, bearing our own wounds transformed and glorified.

Yet there is still a further lesson to be learned, before we even move to resurrection. The account of the Passion which we read on Good Friday is always St. John's, and for John the Passion itself is a glory. From His first encounter with His captors in the Garden, where the latter are confused and fall to the ground, to His final words from the Cross, Jesus is in control. He is directing events.

And so today we can trust Him to direct events still, as He reigns from the Cross, directing from His pierced body this wounded, struggling Body of Christ which we are. Sorrow is ours at our own woundedness, yet trust is also ours that these very wounds will be glorious.

Reflection 17   Acts10:34,37-43, Ps.117:1-2,16-17,22-23, Col.3:1-4, Jn.20:1-9

An Easter homily

I don't know whether you have noticed, but there is a lot of running going on this morning. Mary Magdalene runs to Peter and John, and then these two have a race to the tomb which John wins. Actually, you get the impression that he won by a distance—he has had time to see the linen cloths before Peter arrives, though I suspect that when he bent down, which is when he saw the linen cloths, he may simply have been trying to get his breath back.

It wasn't until my mid 20s that I was bitten by the running bug, but when it does bite, it bites hard, and for the next twenty years, running was my chief recreation until I found that anno Domini was starting to run faster than I could.

There is something hugely liberating about a good long run, with your feet pounding, your blood pumping, hills being conquered, and fresh air filling your lungs. When you are running well, you feel fully alive. Perhaps cyclists have the same feeling: I have not the slightest desire to attempt to find out.

But "fully alive" is the phrase which should define every Christian. Indeed, St. Irenaeus, one of the early Church Fathers, saw this as the hallmark of our relationship with God. "The glory of God is human beings fully alive" he said, echoing Jesus' own words "I have come that they may have life, and have it to the full".

Today of all days we are given permission to be fully alive. The tomb is empty. Christ is risen. Life is totally victorious. Yet this could not have happened, had death not come first. Jesus the Christ was, of course, alive before His death, but death still lurked in the wings. Until He had embraced death, entered into death, passed through death, and emerged on the other side, His life was not complete, was not total, was not final. The race was not won, the enemy was not conquered, full life was not yet achieved.

The empty tomb is essential to the story of life: it gives life its full meaning. The cloths which the disciples see in the tomb are signs that Christ had been there, that Good Friday had not been a dream, a nightmare. Peter and John study these cloths, note their positions, and try to fathom their meaning, a meaning which dawns first upon John: He has been here; He said He would rise from the dead; He has been as good as His word. And that very evening, they would receive the full vindication of their faith, as Christ stood among them in the Upper Room.

Christ is alive, fully alive, with a life seized in His passage through death; and He invites us to share in that fullness of life with Him. Last night, at the Easter Vigil, we heard St. Paul say "When we were baptised, we went into the tomb with Him, and joined Him in death," so we don't need to wait for our own death to be fully alive in Christ.

He has done the dying for us: our part in that death was our baptism, so now, NOW, we live His risen life. Yes our bodies will run more slowly, and they will die, but that is a stage along the road. The race is already won, victory has already been achieved. Because Christ has left the tomb, the tomb which we entered by our baptism, we are fully alive now.

So live today to the full. Run for miles, if your legs and lungs are still up to it: if not, give a hop, skip, and jump. And if even that is beyond you, let your mind run free. Eat good food, drink good ale, because Christ is risen, and He has made you fully alive—today, yes, but every day of your life, on this earth, and in eternity.

Reflection 18 Acts 2:42-47, Ps.117:2-4,13-15,22-24, 1Ptr.1:3-9, Jn.20:19-31

Seeing and believing

Good old Thomas! What a thoroughly modern character he is. "Unless I can see, unless I can touch, unless I can feel, unless I can have it scientifically demonstrated and proved, I refuse to believe." Isn't that exactly the standpoint of so many people today? Isn't that the basis of the so-called new atheism, which isn't new at all, but the same tired old atheism re-heated?

Does it work? Well, only up to a point. What are the really important things in life? What are the factors on which we base our lives, the considerations which get us out of bed in the morning, and which bring out the best in us, making us truly human? Well, love, for starters. How do you see love? How do you touch love? How do you measure love scientifically? Unless you reduce love to the biological imperative to reproduce, and therefore to preserve the species, you have to admit that it goes far beyond the provable, the measurable, and the merely scientific.

Generosity, self-sacrifice, compassion, trust, faith, hope—these are the things which define humanity, yet none of them fits under a microscope, submits to mathematical calculation, is demonstrable in the laboratory. The demand for scientific proof is fine as far as it goes, but for a truly human life it doesn't go far enough, as any honest atheist would have to admit. Thomas is a modern man in demanding his scientific proof, but he is also a modern man--an honest modern man—in ultimately being drawn beyond the limits of the purely demonstrable.

"Blessed are they who have not seen and yet believe" says the risen Christ, setting the measure for the truly human life. We accept the evidence of our senses, we follow the scientific arguments, we rejoice in the expansion of demonstrable knowledge, but if we are to be truly human, we take that step further: we surrender ourselves in love, we commit ourselves in hope, and we journey into the unknown in faith.

"My Lord and my God" are Thomas's final words on the subject, words which show him to be willing to take that further, fully rational, deeply human step of committing himself to faith, hope, and love. The scientific has taken him as far as it can. He has seen, he has touched, he has felt, and on that basis he feels the need to go further, to make that statement of faith, that leap of faith, towards which the experiment points him but which it cannot absolutely demonstrate, and so, not only on his own behalf, but on behalf of the Church throughout the ages, he says "My Lord and my God".

In those words, Thomas gives us a definition, a summary, of the person of Christ, a definition and a summary to which he has been inexorably led. Without his scientific rationalism, he couldn't have come so far: it provides the launching pad for his final step of faith. It provides us, too, with a basis for our own faith. As another Thomas, the thirteenth century Dominican St. Thomas Aquinas wrote in his great Eucharistic hymn,

"I am not like Thomas, wounds I cannot see,

But can plainly call Thee Lord and God as he".

It is no coincidence that we use those words silently as we gaze on the Eucharistic Christ at the elevation of the host and then of the chalice at every Mass. Like Thomas the Apostle we see—we see the elements over which the words of consecration have been spoken—but also like him we take the step of faith, and we pray "My Lord and my God".

Were you brought up to pray those words silently at the elevation? If you were, renew your commitment to that practice. If you weren't, then take up the practice now. Every time the bell rings, and the priest holds up the consecrated host, the Body of Christ, and the chalice containing the Blood of Christ, repeat mentally those words of Thomas "My Lord and my God".

To do that is to be truly modern. It is to accept the principles of scientific rationalism, but then, rationally, logically, wisely, to do the human thing and move beyond them, making that step of faith in the presence of the risen Christ which alone gives complete meaning to life, the universe, and everything.

Reflection 19   Acts 2:14,22-33, Ps. 15:1-25,7-11, 1Ptr.1:17-21, Lk.24:13-35

We are the Young Ones

Even after a couple of years, the new Mass translation still grates in places. There are times when the sharpness of a prayer becomes lost in a thicket of words. That is true of the opening prayer of today's Mass where the opening prayer used to thrill me every time I read it. It ran "You have made us your sons and daughters and restored the joy of our youth". In other words, "You have made us young again" and I always had the mental image of us all leaping and laughing and being children again.

That prayer, in its 1970s form, reminded us of an important truth: that age isn't a matter of years but of attitude, and, deep down, a matter of how we respond to the promptings of the Holy Spirit; how strongly we allow the Holy Spirit, who dwells within us through our baptism and confirmation, to set us mentally hopping, skipping, and jumping.

I am told that the late Mgr. Gregory Turner, who remained a young man in attitude to the day of his death, used to reminisce about the time when he and I were together at St. Mary's, Morecambe, in the 1980s and, in his words, had the parish "jumping". By that, I think that he meant that the parish was very much alive, but I love the picture conjured up by that word "jumping", as I try to envisage the sober citizens of Morecambe leaping and bouncing through the church and along the prom. I hope that observers, seeing this parish, would say that Claughton is jumping: the more we open ourselves to the Holy Spirit, the better we shall jump.

Another character who comes to mind is Mgr. McReavy, the moral theologian of my seminary days. "Bomber" was in his seventies when I knew him, but he was still a young man because he was interested in everything and everybody, driven by a deep relationship with God. I recall revisiting the seminary some time after my ordination, and receiving a thump in the back which almost drove me through the window. It was Mgr. McReavy, overwhelming with questions: Where are you now? How is it going? How are you keeping?

On the other hand, we all know people who seem to have been born old, people for whom everything is negative, everything is wearisome, everything is worse than it used to be, and getting worse all the time. You can find this attitude even among people who are young in years, but who find everything BORING, that most depressing of adjectives which always says more about the person using it than about the situation about which it is used.

I can't help feeling that our real youthfulness is a matter of depth. The deeper our spiritual life, the stronger our relationship with God, the younger we are likely to become. If we live life on the surface, constantly looking for superficial excitement, for relief from boredom, we may be satisfied for a time, but it won't last. Deep relationships, with God and with other people, are the real key to youth.

And at its deepest, this involves a deep relationship with Jesus Christ in the Mass. Those people who complain that Mass is boring, and who go off in search of a livelier, more instantly self-gratifying form of worship, are missing the opportunity of the deepest of all encounters with God, the fullest means of rejuvenation. They may find surface satisfaction, but they are in danger of sacrificing going deep in favour of getting high, of mistaking the superficial for the ultimately real.

In the Mass, the living God who is eternally young draws us into His death and resurrection, the fullest source of life, of energy, of youth. That is what the two Emmaus disciples of today's Gospel discover, as the risen Christ celebrates Mass with them.

Did you realise, by the way, that what you heard described in the Gospel was a celebration of Mass? The risen Christ explains the scriptures: that is the first part of the Mass, the Liturgy of the Word. This causes their hearts to burn within them, as they meet Christ in His word, and are drawn to a deeper understanding. But recognition comes with the Liturgy of the Eucharist, the second part of the Mass, when Jesus takes, blesses, and breaks the bread, and then disappears from their sight, because He is now present in the bread which has become His body.

Suddenly, the two disciples are young again, and they dash back to Jerusalem to share the good news. If we are willing, like them, to meet the risen Christ in His word, and then in the sacrament and sacrifice of His body broken and His blood poured out, we too have the prospect of becoming young again. "You have made us your sons and daughters and restored the joy of our youth."

Reflection 20   Acts 2:14,36-41, Ps.22, 1 Ptr.2:20-25, Jn.10:1-10

Smelly sheep

As you probably know, the Sunday readings come around in a three year cycle, and I have worked it out that the first homily I ever gave must have been on these very readings, thirteen cycles ago, in other words, thirty nine years ago, at Sacriston, in Co. Durham, shortly before being ordained a deacon.

If I searched hard enough, I could probably find that original homily, buried among a mass of papers. I wouldn't particularly want to, because I hope that my understanding may have moved on in those thirty nine years, and that I may be given inspiration by the Holy Spirit every time I look at the scriptures anew. On the other hand, I have discovered more than once, when I think that I have come up with a fresh idea, that if I do look back over homilies past, I find that I had the same idea three years earlier, and six, and nine, perhaps going all the way back to thirty nine. As Ecclesiastes said, "There is nothing new under the sun".

Nonetheless, let us take a look at today's readings, and see how they speak to us today: how, please God, the Holy Spirit will guide us in our understanding of them TODAY.

Sheep and shepherds feature prominently in the psalm, the second reading, and the Gospel. This may carry our minds back to Holy Week, when we contemplated Jesus as the Paschal Lamb, led to the slaughter, saving us by His blood, as the blood of the lambs, smeared on the doorposts, saved the Israelites at the first Passover.

The understanding of Jesus as the lamb is very strong in every celebration of Mass, as He is held up before us, just before communion, as "the Lamb of God who takes away the sins of the world". In today's readings, though, there is a shifting of roles, as Jesus is presented as the shepherd—with us, not as innocent lambs, but as rather gormless sheep, going astray, needing to be called back, to be sheltered, to be led.

Are we gormless? We would probably want to deny it, but if we look at the world, and consider the crazy and the wicked things being done by human beings every day; and if we look at ourselves, and think of the daft mistakes we have made and still make, we may not be so confident. The leading, the guidance, the protection of the Good Shepherd who is Christ are things which we constantly need.

So how does the Good Shepherd meet our needs? Unlike western farmers, whose method, as far as I know, is to round up the sheep from behind, and to drive them ahead, the Middle Eastern shepherd goes in front, relying on the sheep to follow. That involves a fair amount of trust on the shepherd's part, and a recognition of, and reliance on, his voice on the part of the sheep. How does that translate into our lives, as we seek to follow the Good Shepherd?

Firstly, I should think, it demands of us that we know the Shepherd, so that we recognise His voice. That means that we have to spend time getting to know Him, allowing Him to speak to us in the scriptures, drawing closer to Him through time given to prayer. If we do that, we will have the desire and the confidence to keep following, not to lag behind or to wander off.

There is another factor, though, which Our Lord introduces when He extends the parable, speaking of Himself as the gate. Apparently, at night, the Palestinian shepherds of Jesus' time would lie down across the entrance of the sheepfold, forming a human barrier. Wild animals would be put off by the human scent, and so would be deterred from attacking the sheep, while the sheep on the other hand, recognising the scent of their own shepherd, would happily hop over him, in and out of the pen.

That opens up a few trains of thought. Firstly, there is the same call to know Our Lord and to trust Him. Pope Francis has called on bishops and priests, who share in Christ's role as shepherd, to "live with the smell of the sheep", but this parable calls on the sheep to live with the smell of the shepherd. Again, a deep knowledge of Jesus the Christ is inferred: whether the sheep are also called to live with smelly pastors I leave to your imagination.

One aspect of Our Lord's words which, I am sure, did not strike me on that long ago Sunday in Co. Durham is His reference to those who enter through Him "going freely in and out", which He couples with His statement "I have come so that they may have life and have it to the full". This seems to imply a much more relaxed attitude than we have sometimes been used to in the Church, a mutual trust between sheep and shepherd which allows the sheep a great measure of freedom while they grow to maturity through a confident relationship with the Lord.

Contrast this with the atmosphere of fear which had begun to predominate in the Church before Pope Benedict's awesomely courageous decision to resign, an atmosphere in which the Congregation for the Doctrine of the Faith (nee the Inquisition) was actively encouraging the reporting to Rome of anybody whose attitude could be interpreted, however remotely, or unfairly, as "dissent". Such reporting has been forbidden by the present Holy Father, who has been inspired by the example of the Good Shepherd Himself, who seeks to draw the sheep through loving trust, and who came so that you and I, and all His people "should have life, and have it to the full".

Reflection 21   Acts 6:1-7, Ps.32:1-2,4-5, 1 Ptr.2:4-9, Jn.14:1-12

How special are you?

Are you anything special? "No" sez you. "Yes" says God, and St. Peter reiterates it in today's second reading: "You are a chosen race, a royal priesthood, a consecrated nation, a people set apart".

Every human being is special of course, being created in the image and likeness of God, but we who have been baptised into Christ are extra special. There was a baptism at Claughton last Sunday, and I was struck, as I always am, by the prayer which accompanies the anointing with chrism, the Messianic oil: "As Christ was anointed priest, prophet and king, so may you live always as a member of His body, sharing everlasting life."

There are echoes in that prayer of St. Peter's claim that you are a royal priesthood. One of the Reformation controversies focused on the priesthood of all believers. The Reformers concentrated on this to the extent, in some cases, of denying an ordained priesthood, which caused the Church to react by stressing the importance of ordination. Like many arguments, it became blown up out of all proportion.

In fact, the Church believes in the priesthood of all believers, but also distinguishes the ordained priesthood as drawn from the universal priesthood to provide a particular witness and to perform particular functions. It is not, as the late Cardinal Heenan once claimed that "You are little priests and I am a big priest", but that we are all priests, and I have been ordained from among you to focus your priestly offering in a sacramental way.

What does it mean to say that you are a royal priesthood, to claim that you have been anointed in Christ to share His role as priest, prophet, and king? A priest is someone who offers sacrifice, and you, by your baptism, are called to offer the sacrifice of your lives to Christ. Everything you do, provided it is not sinful, you do as a member of Christ's body, the Church, and so every action of yours is a priestly action.

I hope that you make a morning offering to God each day, consecrating to God everything you will do and undergo during that day: that is a priestly action, making your whole day priestly. And then in the Mass, you bring the offering of your daily lives and unite it to the offering of Christ Himself who makes present, through the words and actions of the ordained priest, His offering of Himself on Calvary.

But why a "Royal" priesthood? Remember again that post-baptismal prayer: "As Christ was anointed priest, prophet, and KING." Like Melchizedek in the Old Testament,

Christ is both priest and King, and both His priesthood and His kingship reached fulfilment in His self-offering on the Cross: Christ was a king who reigned in dying, and whose life was a life of service. So the baptised are a royal priesthood whose royalty is expressed in service, in dying to self, and reaches its high point when we unite our self-sacrifice to the sacrifice of Christ in the Mass.

In this priestly, prophetic, and royal unity with Christ lie the answers to the questions posed by Thomas and Philip. "How can we know the way?" asks Thomas. "Show us the Father" demands Philip. And the answer comes back "I am the way". If we are living out that unity with Christ which we received in our baptism, then we are on the way, we are living the truth, we are sharing the life of Christ who is the way the truth, and the life.

If we are recognising the presence of Christ both in the events of our lives and in the sacrament and sacrifice of the Mass, then we are seeing the Father to whom our offering is made. And because Christ, ascended to the Father, is directing the work of His priestly people, and so building the Kingdom of God, then Christ can say that we are doing a greater work than He did during His time on earth, because He is now giving heavenly direction to that work.

Are you anything special? Indeed you are, because you have been baptised into the body of Christ who is priest, prophet, and king, and so have become in Him a royal priesthood transforming the world, by offering it, along with yourselves, to the Father.

Reflection 22   Acts 8:5,14-17, Ps.65:1-7,16,20, 1Ptr.3:15-18

Breaking the rules

Were you any good at maths? I wasn't naturally good at maths—the subject never came easily—but I was an awkward so-and-so, refusing to be beaten, so I used to spend literally hours on my maths homework until I got the right answers, and eventually I managed a Grade 1 in my maths O-level. (Actually I hear that they are going back to a numbering system for GCSE grades, but they are turning them upside down so that 1 will be the lowest grade, so perhaps I should be quiet about my Grade 1.)

My best subject was Latin, which had something in common with maths, in that they both obeyed strict rules—in which they differed from life, which frequently ignores the rules or flouts them, turning them upside down, coming at us from all sorts of crazy angles, and in the process turning US upside down.

I mention maths because today's Gospel reminds me of a mathematical equation. Our Lord begins "If you love me, you will keep my commandments" and after pursuing His argument He concludes "Anybody who receives my commandments and keeps them will be one who loves me". If x then y: x, therefore y.

All Our Lord's words in between are fairly densely packed. They deal with the giving of the Holy Spirit, who WILL come, but who HAS already come. While promising that the Father will give the Holy Spirit, Jesus also uses the present tense in speaking of the Holy Spirit: "He is with you: He is in you."

In other words, we cannot tie the Holy Spirit down. As Jesus says in another place, the Holy Spirit is like the wind, which blows where it will and, we might add, when it will.

If I were to say to you "When was the Holy Spirit given to the apostles?" you might answer "At Pentecost" and you would be right, but only partly right. Remember Easter Sunday evening when the risen Christ appeared to the disciples in the Upper Room, breathed on them, and said "Receive the Holy Spirit".

"Ah" you may now say, "So the Holy Spirit WAS given at Pentecost, but was first given on Easter Sunday evening". Well, not exactly. Today's Gospel is drawn from Jesus' words at the Last Supper, before both Pentecost and Easter Sunday, yet He says to the apostles, on the subject of the Holy Spirit, "He IS with you: He IS in you". So even before these two occasions, the Holy Spirit is with and in the apostles, purely because He IS the Holy Spirit. He blows where He will, and He isn't bound by any laws, whether of maths or of Latin.

We tend to think that we received the Holy Spirit at our baptism and our confirmation, and we are right, but the Holy Spirit isn't limited to or by sacraments. He comes to us in those sacraments, but He also comes as and when He will. Take the example of the Samaritans in today's First Reading. Peter and John pray for them to receive the Holy Spirit, and, we are told, "Then they laid hands on them, and they received the Holy Spirit".

Indeed they did, and yet the Holy Spirit must have been with them already to inspire them to be baptised, to lead them to accept the word of God. All our good actions are the work of the Holy Spirit who cannot be tied down to rules, logic, times, or seasons.

Back we come then to Our Lord's opening and closing words: "If you love me you will keep my commandments". What are the Lord's commandments? Essentially, they are the commands to love. Remember how Jesus summed up all the commandments under the heading of those which He identified as the first two: "You must love the Lord your God with all your heart, soul, mind, and strength, and you must love your neighbour as yourself".

If we keep these commandments of love, then by definition we are loving the Lord, we are being inspired by the Holy Spirit. Our ability to do this comes from God's love for us, and leads to God's love for us. As Jesus goes on to say, "Anybody who loves me will be loved by my Father, and I shall love them and show myself to them".

In a sense this is a circular argument. More to the point, it is a circular process. God loves us, enabling us to love Him, which causes Him to love us, and to dwell within us. Is it circular, or is it a spiral? I leave that for you to work out.

Finally, what does Our Lord mean by saying "I shall show myself to them"? Maybe it means that He will make us more conscious of His presence, which is always with us. He will help us to see Him in our neighbour, to be more aware that He is with us in our times of prayer, to recognise His activity in the events of our lives, to be conscious of Him even when He seems to be absent, when our prayer is dry and without consolations, when we are called by Him to the Garden of the Agony or to the Cross. We may even find Him in the rules of mathematics or of Latin, but we can guarantee that He will also break the rules.

Reflection 23 *Acts 1:1-11, Ps.46:2-3,6-9, Eph. 1:17-23, Matt.28:16-20*

Don't talk rubbish!

People talk rubbish. I talk rubbish, you talk rubbish, he/she/it talks rubbish, and so on. As you know, I frequently talk rubbish on purpose, and you either laugh or groan, depending on how charitable you are feeling. Sometimes, I have no doubt, I talk rubbish without intending it, and you show immense charity by letting it pass.

One subject on which people frequently talk rubbish without intending it is the period between Ascension and Pentecost. I have heard even highly intelligent people claim that, until the Holy Spirit came upon the apostles at Pentecost, they were cowering in fear in the Upper Room.

If ever you hear anyone say that, thump them, pummel them, box their ears, knock them down, and sit on their heads, because it is utter, unmitigated rubbish. Why do they say it? Largely because the Gospel used at Pentecost is St. John's account of the appearance of the Risen Christ on Easter Sunday evening, when the disciples were indeed cowering in fear until the Risen One breathed on them and said "Receive the Holy Spirit". Because this Gospel is used at Pentecost, people believe that it refers to Pentecost, forgetting that they previously heard it read on Low Sunday.

Why on earth would the apostles, and the rest of the disciples, have been fearful after the Ascension? As St. Luke tells us today, in that reading from the Acts of the Apostles, the Risen Christ had spent forty days repeatedly appearing to them and telling them about the Kingdom of God. He had spent all that time encouraging them, putting fresh heart into them, which is what "encourage" literally means (from the Latin "cor" meaning "heart").

And then what? "He had told them," says St. Luke, "not to leave Jerusalem, but to wait there for what the Father had promised" and He explained that this would be baptism with the Holy Spirit.

So, in other words, when the Holy Spirit descended at Pentecost, it was not upon frightened people, but upon people who were doing what the Lord had told them, waiting, and not only waiting, but praying. If you look a couple of pages on in the Mass book, to the Seventh Sunday of Easter, (which we don't now keep, since the bishops moved Ascension to Sunday) you will find the next three verses of the Acts of the Apostles, which tell us, not only that "they joined in continuous prayer" but also that Our Lady was with them. Frightened? Rubbish! Nonsense! Gobbledygook!

There was no fear associated with the Ascension, though there was a degree of puzzlement. The apostles couldn't work out the practicalities of what had happened, and they stood there staring. They were in danger of becoming bogged down by trivia—and we can do the same. Where exactly did Jesus go, and how? "Don't worry about that" say the angels. "That's not the point. Don't stand around gawping. Get on with the job. Do what He told you. Go and prepare for the outpouring of the Spirit." And so they do.

So what about us? What are we supposed to do? Like the apostles we should set about praying, with the help of Our Lady, for a new outpouring of the Holy Spirit. We should pray intensely for the Holy Spirit to be poured out afresh on us, on the Church, on the whole of creation.

To what end? For what purpose? Our Lord gives the answer to that immediately before He ascends. It is in order to be His witnesses, "indeed to the ends of the earth".

"Oo-er!" you may say. "How on earth will we do that?" especially in these days when people are increasingly indifferent to Jesus Christ, if not actively hostile?

I don't think we need to worry too much about the hows and the wherefores. If we genuinely trust in the Holy Spirit, if we sincerely pray for the outpouring of that Spirit, He will take care of the details. Two sayings, separated by seven centuries, but essentially making an identical point, spring to mind.

One of them is attributed to St. Francis of Assisi, whether correctly or not I do not know. Francis is alleged to have told his followers: "Preach the Gospel by every means possible. If necessary, even use words." Whether he said that or not, the second quotation, from Pope Paul VI, is certainly genuine, because it is in his encyclical "Evangelii Nuntiandi" for anyone to read. In this document, written in the mid 1970s, Pope Paul wrote "People today listen more to witnesses than to teachers, and if they listen to teachers, it is because they are also witnesses".

In other words, don't talk about the Gospel: live the Gospel. Don't talk about Jesus Christ: let Jesus Christ live in you. If you are striving to do that, you will be His witnesses: you will make Him known. By being the people whom you are called to be, you will already have influenced more people than you will ever know: you will have shown the face of Jesus Christ to them. Pray and be! In that way, you will fulfil the task which Jesus Christ left us at His Ascension, and you will do it far more effectively than any words—though words may come in handy, provided you don't talk rubbish.

Reflection 24   <u>Acts 2:1-11, Ps.103:1,24,29-31, 1 Cor.12:3-7,12-13,</u>
<u>Jn.20:19-23</u>

Did you receive the Spirit?

Can you speak foreign languages? I daresay that there are some of you who can get by, or who are even fluent, in one or two. With my O-level French (1965) I can read notices, and can even have a go at the newspaper, but when it comes to speaking, I have to rehearse very carefully what I am going to say, and when the other person replies, I am stymied.

Have I then not received the Holy Spirit? Or was the giving of the Spirit simply a once-for-all event at Pentecost, to be remembered as something past, but not necessarily relevant today?

To cure us of that way of thinking, I suspect that we have to look more closely at the other readings of today's liturgy, rather than simply focus on the Pentecost event in isolation.

The Gospel recalls the Easter Sunday evening appearance of the risen Christ in the Upper Room, when He breathed on the disciples and said "Receive the Holy Spirit", giving them the power to forgive sins. That was a very different giving of the Holy Spirit from the wind and fire of Pentecost, a gentle wafting of the Spirit into frightened and troubled people, an inbreathing which gave them an immense gift, the gift of forgiving sins.

Have you received that gift? Indeed you have. As an ordained priest, I have received the gift of forgiving sins sacramentally, in the name of God and of the whole Church, of reconciling sinners with the Body of Christ which is the Church; but you, as members of that priestly people which is the Church have also been given the Spirit so that you can show to others, in your everyday lives, and communicate to others, the forgiveness which Christ brings.

Every time you forgive someone who has annoyed or upset you; every time you refuse to hold onto a grudge; every time you are positive in a situation in which you could grumble or moan, you are using a gift of the Holy Spirit; you are exercising your royal priesthood as a member of the Body of Christ; you are extending God's forgiveness into that situation, granting it to that person.

You have indeed received the Holy Spirit, and you have received the gifts of the Spirit. And if you remain in any doubt, take a good look at today's Second Reading. "No one can say Jesus is Lord" states St. Paul, "unless they are under the influence of the Holy

Spirit". Do you say that Jesus is Lord? You say it several times every time you come to Mass. "Glory to you, Lord," "Praise to you, Lord Jesus Christ," " Lord, I am not worthy", to say nothing of your silent prayers—"My Lord and my God" at the elevation, and your prayers of thanksgiving after receiving the Body and Blood of Christ. It is the Holy Spirit who enables you to say those prayers, to make those statements, no less than it was the Holy Spirit who gave gifts to the Pentecost disciples.

St. Paul goes on to drive the point home. "There is a variety of gifts but always the same Spirit...working in all sorts of different ways in different people...The particular way in which the Spirit is given to each person is for a good purpose."

So in what ways has the Spirit been given to you? What are your gifts? (And please don't tell me that you don't have any.) I see an abundance of gifts in this parish: musical gifts; gifts of proclaiming the word of God or of administering the Blood of Christ; gifts of organisation; practical gifts for making or repairing or for drawing out the beauty of gardens; gifts of flower arranging or of cleaning; gifts of listening, of supporting, of caring for others, or of bringing up a family; gifts of kindness and of friendship, of patience and generosity; gifts of time made available for service in great or small ways.

One gift of immense importance is the gift of prayer, which doesn't necessarily mean that prayer comes easily. It means that you are prepared to struggle with prayer, to live through distractions, to persevere when the going gets tough and everything seems dry and unrewarding. That is definitely a gift of the Holy Spirit. In a reading from St. Paul to the Romans prescribed for a Pentecost Vigil we are told "When we cannot choose words in order to pray properly, the Spirit Himself expresses our plea in a way which could never be put into words".

Why were the Pentecost disciples given the gift of tongues, of foreign languages? It was not so that they could impress one another, or the listening crowds; it was so that they could express the marvels of God, so that they could continue Christ's work of building the Kingdom of God. You and I have received the Holy Spirit for precisely the same reason, so that we can proclaim the marvels of God by our words and by our way of life, so that we can work to build the Kingdom. The gifts of the Spirit are our gifts, and Pentecost is our feast.

Reflection 25 — Deut. 8:2-3,14-16, Ps.147:12-15,19-20, 1Cor.10:16-17, Jn.6:51-58

A homily for Corpus Christi

Some of you may know Sister Michaela from Hyning. We go back a long way, as Sr.M. was a pupil at Our Lady's High School, Lancaster, when I was chaplain there thirty years ago.

Sr. Michaela and I also have something in common, in that we both have rather weird faculties of memory, with a knack for remembering all sorts of minor things which occurred decades ago. I was reminded of this a few weeks ago, on my most recent visit to Hyning, when Sr. M recalled a homily which I gave during a school Mass on the feast of Corpus Christi, when she was about fifteen.

In the course of the homily, I mentioned that people, and especially young people, will often say that Mass is boring. I then pointed beyond the windows of the assembly hall, where the Mass was being celebrated, in the direction of the Castle, and I reminded the pupils—or perhaps, informed them, as they probably weren't aware of it—that over the centuries fifteen people were imprisoned in the Castle and then dragged through the streets to the Low Moor where they were hanged, drawn and quartered purely because they were determined to share in the Mass whether as priests or as laypeople, because the Mass was more important to them than life itself.

Why was the Mass so important? Because it was, and is, the ultimate meeting point with Jesus Christ: because in the Mass we do indeed eat the flesh of the Son of Man and drink His blood: because we receive the living God into ourselves, so that He becomes part of us, flesh of our flesh and bone of our bone, united with us more closely than we are with ourselves.

I pointed all this out and concluded by asking, rather heatedly "How the hang can that be boring?" a question which I would still ask today. Whether it made any impression on anybody else I have no idea, but at least Sr. Michaela has remembered it for thirty years.

When it comes down to hey-lads-hey, it is the Mass, the Eucharist, the Body and Blood of Christ, which defines us as Catholics. Other Christian share with us belief in the Trinity, faith in Jesus Christ, prayer, the scriptures, but what marks us out, even more than the primacy of the Pope, is our Eucharistic belief and practice. All Christians have some sort of belief in the Eucharist, but apart from the Orthodox and a number of High Church Anglicans (though an increasing proportion of Anglicans, it has to be said) only we have that complete adherence to, and emphasis on, those words of Jesus Christ about eating His flesh and drinking His blood.

I have quoted before, that television documentary from the early 1970s about the Catholic Church which the presenter concluded with the statement, "When you talk to Catholics, the phrase which keeps cropping up is "the Body of Christ": the Body of Christ which is the Eucharist, and the Body of Christ which is the Church". That TV presenter had it exactly right: the Body of Christ is what makes us, and the Body of Christ is who and what we are. Our forefathers and foremothers were prepared to die for that truth. Let us put aside any thought of boredom, and live by and for that same truth.

Reflection 26   Acts 12:1-11, P.33:2-9, 2 Tim.4:6-8,17-18, Matt.16:13-19

Flawed geniuses—Saints Peter and Paul

If you were founding a Church, would you choose to found it on the basis of Saints Peter and Paul? If you were calling disciples, would Peter and Paul be among the front runners? Somehow, I doubt it.

Let's look at the evidence. Peter was impetuous, a bit of a loudmouth, better at promising than at delivering, with more than a hint of cowardice about him. Paul was difficult, prickly, not the sort of person you would choose to go on holiday with: and if you did go on holiday with him, it's odds on you would have been returning home sooner than you had planned.

Think of some of Peter's failures. He sees Jesus walking on the lake. "Lord, if it is you," he cries, "bid me come to you across the water". Yet when he begins to walk, his nerve fails him, and he has to be rescued by the Lord, who chides him for his lack of faith.

Then, immediately after the incident in today's Gospel, when Our Lord has named him as the rock on which the Church is to be built, he opens his mouth and puts his foot in it. Jesus begins to speak about His impending Passion, so Peter sets out to prove what a good leader of the Church he will be, by taking control of the situation. "No, no," he interrupts, "that isn't going to happen," the implication being that the Lord can rely on him to prevent it, just about as unfortunate a misreading of his role as you can imagine.

How many times does he promise to stand by Jesus, to die for Him if the occasion demands it? And then how drastically does he let Him down? Falling asleep in Gethsemane, when the Lord has need of his support, cutting off the ear of the High Priest's servant—the wrong reaction again; finally suffering complete failure by his three fold denial, as the crowing cock mocks the total collapse of the man of straw.

Even after that, and after his tears of repentance, there were slips and stumbles to come. Peter was too slow on the uptake to understand why the Lord questioned him three times about his love, failing to grasp that a threefold assertion was needed to offset the threefold denial. Finally, there was his moral cowardice when he abandoned his principles and stopped eating with the Gentile Christians, earning a holier-than-thou rebuke from Paul.

What about Paul? Leaving aside his pre-conversion zeal in persecuting the Church, there are enough charges against him in his days as a disciple to cause eyebrows to rise and lips to purse. Take his criticism of Peter for starters. Certainly Peter was in the wrong in failing to stick to his guns in the face of criticism from Jewish Christians, but what about Paul's reaction? Our Lord left very clear instructions that correction was to be carried out privately and quietly, a principle totally abandoned by Paul as he brags in the Letter to the Galatians of his moral superiority in giving Peter a dressing down. I have always felt that Peter would have done us all a favour if he had taken Paul round the back and given him a good smack in the mouth, thus taking him down a peg or three.

Yet Paul himself was extremely touchy if he was criticised, displaying what could almost be described as temper tantrums in some of his letters, and giving hints that he wasn't immune to the very fault which he condemns in Peter, as he struggles to rebut the charge that he was strong in his letters, but weak when he encountered people face to face.

And isn't there something questionable in the character of someone who falls out with one companion after another: Demas, Mark, even Barnabas, who had worked so hard to ensure Paul's acceptance by the Church at large? Over all, I think it is fair to say that Paul was not someone you would have wanted your daughter to marry.

Yet these two deeply flawed characters formed the foundation stones of the Church, Peter recognised as the first Pope, and Paul spreading the Gospel throughout the Mediterranean world. The Church built on these bases has endured through two millennia, not without stumbles, failures, and grave sins: and the Gospel has been preached the length and breadth of this planet. Our presence in this church today is testimony to the work of Saints Peter and Paul—and to God's ability to write straight with crooked lines.

Maybe that last point is of particular importance to us. Do you and I have flaws in our characters? Without a doubt. Would Christ have chosen any of us as foundation stones for His Church? Would He heck! But has He chosen us, with all our faults, to be members of that Church, to play our part in building the Kingdom and spreading the Gospel? Indeed He has! Can we wriggle out of our responsibilities on the basis of our weaknesses, our inadequacies, our sins? 'Fraid not. If God could build a whole Church on such flawed characters as Peter and Paul, then He can certainly achieve His purposes with and through us, and we have no excuses which will allow us to evade our responsibilities, to ignore our own individual call.

Reflection 27   Zech.9:9-10, Ps.144:1-2,8-11,13-14, Rom.8:9,11-13, Matt:25-30

The pierced heart

It is a little surprising that, having moved out of June, the month of the Sacred Heart, we are confronted with readings which are usually associated with the Feast of the Sacred Heart, as Zechariah prophesies the arrival of a humble king, and Jesus speaks of Himself as gentle and humble in heart.

Devotion to the Sacred Heart of Jesus owes much of its popularity to the visions granted to St. Margaret Mary Alacoque, a seventeenth century French nun, but as today's readings show, it is also deeply scriptural. The Heart of Jesus in which the troubled are invited to find rest, and whose humility we are called to imitate, calls to us across the millennia from the compassionate ministry of the Lord, and from the Cross, where that heart was pierced by the soldier's lance.

Two key words spring from our consideration of the Heart of Jesus, the Sacred Heart, both of which occur in today's scriptures: these words are humility and compassion.

The king in Zechariah's prophecy is described as humble, and the sign of his humility is his choice of mount, not a war horse, but a donkey, a sign of peace. Our Lord describes Himself as gentle and humble in heart, and thanks His Father for revealing the mysteries of the Kingdom to "mere children", the human equivalents of Zechariah's donkey, unregarded, unsophisticated, willing to be guided and to learn.

Elsewhere, Our Lord demands that those who follow Him must be compassionate, suffering with a suffering world. He claims this as a quality of God Himself—"be compassionate as your Father is compassionate"—and it is shown most fully in the Incarnation, God taking on our human flesh, suffering all that is part of human experience. The Christ who is presented to us in statues of, and devotion to, the Sacred Heart, is the compassionate Christ, the Christ whose heart was broken both literally and metaphorically by human suffering and human sin.

One of the most powerful pieces of writing on devotion to the Sacred Heart comes from Karl Rahner, the twentieth century German Jesuit theologian, who exerted a profound influence on the thinking of the Second Vatican Council. At first sight, this is surprising, as Rahner was certainly one of the "learned and the clever". His brother Hugo, also a Jesuit, used to claim that he was going to spend his retirement translating Karl's theological writings into German, the point of the joke being that they were written in German, but a German so abstruse that not even a German could understand them.

Yet Karl Rahner was living proof that the learned and the clever can also be humble. The story is told of his visiting a former classmate, the parish priest of a country parish, and finding him in bed with flu. "Don't worry" said Karl, "I will say your Sunday Mass for you." "That's very kind," replied his friend," but for goodness' sake don't preach. These are simple folk: they won't understand a word you say."

Yet when it came to the time for the homily, Karl felt that he had to say something to break the word for the people, and so, in spite of his friend's warning, he went ahead and preached. Afterwards, an old peasant woman approached him. "Father" she said, "You must be a very simple priest, because you spoke straight to our hearts. Now our parish priest is a lovely man. He only has one fault: when he preaches, no one can understand a word he says."

Karl Rahner speaks of Jesus as "the man with the pierced heart", and says that devotion to the Sacred Heart means that we must become men and women of pierced hearts, pierced with love for God, and for our suffering brothers and sisters. That is compassion, that is "suffering with" that is truly coming to the Heart of Jesus, allowing ourselves to be pierced by that same wound of love which pierced the Sacred Heart.

Another factor presented to us by Zechariah is the peacemaker's role. His king is victorious and triumphant, but he spurns the trappings of a warrior and, in his humility, establishes peace. We think of Jesus' fulfilment of Zechariah's prophecy as He entered Jerusalem on a donkey at the beginning of Passover Week, but also of how His proclamation of peace was, and continues to be, rejected, not least in the region where He spent His earthly life.

As people devoted to the Sacred Heart, we must work and pray for peace, seeking to build peace where we can actively do so, never tiring in our prayers for peace where activity is beyond our grasp. Humble, compassionate, tireless for peace: if and only if we are striving to be those things can we truly claim to have devotion to the Sacred Heart.

Reflection 28   <u>Is.55:10-11, Ps.64:10-14, Rom.8:18-23,</u>
<u>Matt.13:1-23</u>

What kind of soil?

What kind of soil are you, then? What kind am I? Are you hard, rocky ground that nothing and no one can penetrate? "I am a rock, I am an island" Simon and Garfunkel used to sing: "I touch no one and no one touches me". Do you know all the answers? Do you have everything sussed? No need for the scriptures to trouble you. No openings for growth, for movement, for progress: in reality, no room for God.

Or are you shallow soil, quick to become enthusiastic, but equally quick to lose interest? In my time at the Diocesan Residential Youth Centre, I used constantly to warn the young people who came on courses and who became filled with enthusiasm, that the acid test would come when they returned home. Would they retain their enthusiasm to the extent of being willing to participate in the weekly routine of parish Mass, or was it something which, having flared like a firework, would die away just as quickly? The enthusiasm of those who become caught up in Pentecostal and evangelical worship in preference to the seeming dullness of mainstream religious practice sometimes seems to flow in those sorts of channels.

Maybe you are a crowded, overloaded soil, one of the most common forms of soil today, with too much to do, and too little time to do it in. Mass to be slotted in when you can, among all the other weekend activities: your wristwatch to be regularly consulted as time slips by, until eventually something has to give, and the thing which gives is prayer, Mass, time given to God, and you console yourself with the old cliché "I don't have to go to church to be a good person". AAAAAAAAGH!!!

What has "being a good person" got to do with it? Are you not a child of God, called to live in a deep loving relationship with Him? Do you not have a vocation to be filled with His Spirit, in order to take that Spirit into the world and to transform that creation which, St. Paul tells us, groans with a longing to be set free? Would you be a good person if you never visited the parents who love you, and who long for your time and your presence? And are you truly a good person if you ignore the God whose love and longing for you exceed even those of your earthly mother and father?

What sort of soil are you? What sort of soil am I? Speaking, as I did, of the Youth Centre, the first reading always calls to mind the Tuesday of the First Week of Lent in 1987, when I was leading a course with a group of Fifth Years (Year 11 in new money) from St. Joseph's High School, Workington. On that Tuesday afternoon, we walked up Walla Crag. The winter had been hard, a blanket of snow lay on the fields, and the paths were frozen and rutted, ice on the puddles and the soil like rock. A golden sun beat down from a glorious blue sky, and you could imagine the grass renewing itself under its covering of snow, while the ground which we trod looked and felt as if it would never again turn to mud, though experience told us that it would.

We returned from the walk, and headed to the chapel for Mass: lo and behold, the first reading was that commentary from Isaiah which we have heard today: "As the rain and the snow…"

The rain and the snow WOULD make the earth yield. When the snow melted, the grass would be richer and lusher than ever: eventually, the iron hard earth would soften into pliable brown soil, but this wouldn't happen immediately. It would be a slow and gradual process.

So it is with the penetration of God's word into rich and fruitful soil. It doesn't happen overnight. God needs our openness, our willingness to allow His word to soak into us, to break down the iron hard crust of our resistant hearts; to blanket the dryness of our barren souls, so that, slowly and imperceptibly, He may start to change us, to renew us, to make us fruitful and life-giving, so that we may bear a rich crop for Him.

But we have to give His word time and space to do its work. No time, no space! No need! Yes, wonderful—until I lose interest! None of these responses will work. We need to create some time and some space. We have to recognise our need. We have to remember that sudden enthusiasms often fade and die.

Each day we need some time to be still in God's presence, even if it is only a matter of five or ten minutes: God doesn't ask the impossible. Ideally, we will ponder the scriptures slowly, allowing them to seep into us, as God, speaking through Isaiah, has told us that His word will fruitfully do. At least be attentive to the Mass readings, listening out for the word or phrase which will touch your heart. Then you will recognise that yearning and groaning which we share with creation: then you will begin to share that desire for that freedom, that fruitfulness, that fulfilment, which only God can give.

Reflection 29 **Wis.12:13,16-19, Ps.85:5-6,9-10,15-16, Rom.8:26-27, Matt.13:24-43**

A puzzle from Paul

St. Paul sets us a bit of a puzzle today. "When we cannot choose words" he says, "in order to pray properly..." Yet surely we always have the words in order to pray properly: we have the Our Father. When the apostles asked for a lesson in prayer, that is what Our Lord taught them.

Certainly, the Our Father is at the heart of all prayer. As the early Church Fathers said, any prayer which is incompatible with the Our Father cannot be valid. And if we are struggling in prayer, we can always return to the Our Father and pray it slowly and thoughtfully. It is full of material for meditation, for prayerful pondering.

The story is told of a "Family Day" at Ushaw, the Northern seminary, the year after I had left. At the end of the day, the families gathered in St. Cuthbert's chapel for Mass, and the presiding priest began preaching on the Our Father. After three quarters of an hour of his sermon, the visitors all had to stand up and leave to catch their buses, at which point the preacher was still holding forth on "Thy Kingdom Come".

So we will never exhaust the riches of the Our Father. St. Paul would have known this, so why does he speak of our being unable to choose words?

He is making the point—well, actually, he is making two points. Firstly, he is reminding us that prayer is a gift from God. It is the Holy Spirit who moves us to pray, who enables us to pray, without whom our prayer will be sterile and lifeless. Secondly, he is suggesting that the Holy Spirit will lead us to a level deeper than words, a level at which words become unnecessary, and even a distraction, and our greatest need is to be still and silent in God's presence, allowing the Holy Spirit to move in the depths of our being, to be Himself our communication with the Father.

Ideally, our vocal prayer should be leading us into that depth: that is one reason for our use of repetitive prayer such as the rosary, and litanies, which help to still our minds and hearts by their constant rhythm, so that we can open ourselves to the Spirit's guidance. Stillness in prayer is a gift from God, and one which we should have in mind every time we pray.

Strangely enough, this fits in with the three parables of the Kingdom which Our Lord sets before us in the Gospel, because that same call to stillness can be found in them. There is initial activity—the farmer sows the wheat, the husbandman spreads the mustard seed, the woman kneads the dough—but the essential work is done at a deeper level. Once the seed has been sown, it has to be left alone to germinate, to grow into wheat or a mustard plant: digging it up to check on its development would be disastrous. When the yeast has been thoroughly mixed with the flour, the loaf has to be left in the oven: again, too much opening of the oven door will do more harm than good. It is like that with our prayer: the time comes for us to sink into stillness, allowing the Holy Spirit to do the work.

But what of the weeds growing up with the wheat? Again, the Lord counsels against too much activity. "Let them both grow till the harvest." Don't go rooting too thoroughly or too soon.

That is a lesson which the present Pope has heeded, rapping the knuckles of the heresy hunters, who were anxious to denounce everything which they saw as even the slightest deviation from the paths of orthodoxy. A society, or a Church, which is too anxious to purify itself is heading for trouble: it won't be long before it becomes harsh and unforgiving, before its definition of heresy or dissent becomes so wide that virtually everyone is in danger of being trapped.

The next question, though, is what about ourselves? Aren't there weeds growing within us—weeds of sin—and don't we need to root those out? Perhaps we would be better saying that we should open ourselves to let God root them out. We need to examine our consciences, to recognise our faults, to expose them prayerfully to God's searing and healing love, which will do the job of eliminating the weeds far better than we could. Again the danger of trying to do the job ourselves is that we would become too zealous, either damaging our personalities or becoming horribly self-righteous.

So stillness seems to be a key word today. That is the answer to St. Paul's conundrum about prayer. That is the message of Our Lord's parables. That is implied in the First Reading's insistence on the lenient judgement exercised by God.

Reflection 30   1 Kings 3:5,7-12, Ps.118:57,72,76-77,127-130, Rom.8:28-30, Matt.13:44-52

Tell us about the Kingdom

So, what IS the Kingdom like—the Kingdom of God or, as Matthew invariably puts it, "the Kingdom of Heaven", because he was writing for a predominantly Jewish readership, and Jews do not pronounce the name of God? We have any number of comparisons put before us by Our Lord.

Over the past few weeks we have heard that the Kingdom is like seed which falls on different kinds of soil, that it is like wheat, or a mustard seed, or yeast—the leaven in the lump—or, today, like hidden treasure, a pearl of great price, good quality fish, or a mixture of the new and the old. What do these parables have in common, or again, what different aspects of the Kingdom do they bring to the fore?

It strikes me that, common to most, if not all, of these depictions of the Kingdom, is an element of hiddenness, of silent growth or unrecognised readiness. Seed sinks into the earth and grows unseen: yeast works its way into the dough, and vanishes: the hidden treasure is buried again, until its finder, like the discoverer of the fine pearl, can afford to buy it: the fish flop about in the net until the fisher folk settle down to sort them.

Another factor which stands out in some of the parables is the mixture of good and bad. For every piece of rich soil on which the sown seed lands, there are three types of unfruitful ground. The wheat is contaminated by darnel, and both must be undisturbed until the harvest. The dragnet brings in a haul of all kinds; sprats, inedible fish, and general debris, along with fish of quality.

What might these similarities and differences suggest to us? The hiddenness of the Kingdom comes across very powerfully. God works quietly, in the depths of our being, in the hidden places of the world and of the human heart. People who make a show of religion, or who seek to impose their beliefs either by violence or by condemnations and harsh judgements seem to have missed the true nature of the Kingdom. Even the Church is likely to be at her best when she works quietly and unregarded among the little ones of the world, rather than when she mingles with the high and mighty.

As an illustration of that point, I remember a bishop, some years ago, who was due to attend the Nativity play of the Cathedral Primary School. A few moments before the play was due to begin, he rushed into Cathedral House. "Where are they starting from?" he asked. "I'll just have a word with them, and then I'll have to dash off. There's an ecumenical carol service at the Priory, and I need to be at that."

The Cathedral Dean was taken aback. "But the children and their families are expecting you to be there," he objected. "They will be very disappointed. I really think you should stay."

"No, no. I have to be at the Priory." And he was gone.

I wandered into the back of the Cathedral for the play. It was bursting at the seams with parents, grandparents, mothers' boyfriends, aunts, uncles, and all and sundry. There was a preponderance of shaven heads and leather jackets—and that was only the women. Some were chewing, some were leaping out into the aisle to take photos of their little darlings, and others were waving at them. The phrase came unbidden to mind: "like sheep without a shepherd". Meanwhile, where was the shepherd? Hobnobbing with the high and mighty at the Priory.

I tell that story, not to criticise that particular bishop, or bishops in general, but because we can all forget the true nature of the Kingdom. Over and over again, Our Lord tells us that the Kingdom is growing unseen. It is to be found in the hidden places, and among the unlikely people, rather than in the showpiece liturgies or among the great and the good.

But what about that other aspect of the Kingdom emphasised by these parables? What about the mixture of the good and the bad, and the sorting out which is to happen at the Last Judgement? At a personal level, we need to understand what a combination of the good, the bad, and the ugly there is in us. We need to be constantly open to the healing and transforming grace of God, and to recognise that we will always be in need of Purgatory, whether in this life or the next, but almost certainly both, to separate the wheat from the chaff in us.

As for other people, both in the Church and in the world, we need Solomon's wisdom to leave judgement to God. Our task is to live and to grow alongside others, influencing and being influenced for good, trusting God to strain out the good wheat and the high quality fish in the lives of individuals, in the Church, and in the world.

Reflection 31

Is.55:1-3, Ps.144:8-9,15-18, Rom.8:35,37-39, Matt.14:13-21

Loaves and fishes

We have heard a lot about the Kingdom in recent weeks, whether we think of it as the Kingdom of God or, as Matthew puts it, the Kingdom of Heaven. Today we move from parables of the Kingdom to a sign of the Kingdom, a sign that, with the coming of Jesus, the Kingdom is already present and always shall be, though not yet in its fullness or its glory.

When Our Lord feeds the five thousand with the loaves and the fishes, He is making a statement that the Kingdom of God is here. One feature of the Kingdom is to be the Messianic banquet, when the Messiah sits down with the chosen, the elect, and the saved, to enjoy a magnificent feast. In the Apocalypse, the Book of Revelation, the last book of the Bible, this feast becomes the marriage supper of the Lamb, celebrating the final union of the Christ, the Lamb of God, with His bride, the Church.

The feast of loaves and fishes in the lonely place is, in its way, the first instalment of the heavenly banquet; as the Messiah sits down to eat with those who have followed Him. It can hardly be described as a magnificent meal, yet it is a heavenly meal, since it is a miraculous feeding in the presence of the Christ; a sign of the more wonderful feeding which is to come.

It is also a sign of, and preparation for, something else, namely the Messianic banquet of the Eucharist, the Mass, when the Messiah again eats with His people, this time giving Himself as the miraculous food. The Eucharist, Holy Communion, above all other things, is THE sign of the Kingdom, as we share here and now in the marriage supper of the Lamb, and are reminded, as we do so, that there is more to come. This is the Kingdom, this is the Messianic banquet, but not yet revealed in its glory. The Mass is an anticipation, a preparation, but also a reality: the feeding of the 5,000 is an anticipation of the anticipation, a preparation for the preparation.

It is in the Book of the Prophecies of Isaiah that we find the promise of the Messianic banquet most fully set out. In one place, the prophet looks forward to "a banquet of rich food, a banquet of fine wines": today, we have the promise of water to satisfy the thirsty; of corn, wine and milk offered free. This should ring bells with us, reminding us of the life-giving water of baptism, and of the streams of living water, identified with the Holy Spirit, which Our Lord promised as gushing from His wounded heart. The promise of an eternal covenant points us again towards the Mass, in which we receive the blood of the Covenant poured out by the Saviour and given to us to drink.

Yet we know from painful experience that we are still a long way from the fullness of the Kingdom, from the Kingdom in its glory. There are many people in the world who are hungry and thirsty, there are millions of victims of violence, and there is pain, grief, and suffering in our own lives. As subjects of the Kingdom, the demand is made of us that we strain every nerve to feed the hungry, to liberate the oppressed, to comfort those who suffer.

When Our Lord says to the apostles "Give them something to eat yourselves", He is partly encouraging them to recognise their limitations and their need of Him, but He is also calling on them to push the boundaries, to make an effort beyond meek acceptance of a difficult situation. The feeding of the 5,000 is a religious event, but it is also deeply practical, as all good religion must be: the people in the wilderness have their bodily needs met, as well as their spiritual needs, and Christ's followers are called to care for people's bodies as well as their souls.

As well as caring for others, though, we are also called by St. Paul to care for ourselves. We do become troubled and worried, we endure difficulties and problems of one sort or another. Paul reminds us that these difficulties, however great they may be, cannot separate us from Christ: indeed, they can become the means of closer union with Christ, because they are a sharing in His sufferings. In the darkest of our dark nights, we need to cling to this truth, that in our suffering, Christ is suffering with us, and using our suffering as a sharing in His, to help Him redeem the world. Here, no less than in the quenching of our thirst and the satisfying of our hunger, and of the hunger and thirst of others, the Kingdom of God is present.

Reflection 32

1 Kings 19:9,11-13, Ps.84:9-14, Rom.9:1-5, Matt.14:22-33

Courage in the storm

It's not fair is it? Some weeks there seems to be hardly anything in the readings on which to hang a homily; then there are days like this in which there is too much. St. Paul agonises over the situation of his own Jewish people with regard to salvation—an anxiety which, as we shall hear next week, he was able to resolve to his own satisfaction—while either side of his reading, we have two action-packed episodes concerning, first, Elijah, and then Jesus and Peter.

Let's start with Elijah. He was fleeing from the wicked queen, Jezebel, who had sworn to take his life. He escaped into the wilderness, frightened and depressed, and arrived at Mt. Horeb where, according to tradition, the cave where he took refuge was the very spot at which God had revealed Himself to Moses.

There, Elijah too has an experience of God. What are we to make of it? At first, Elijah passes through times of turmoil, violence, upset. There is a destructive gale which causes chaos, followed by an earthquake and a fire, but Elijah recognises God only when there is stillness and quiet. Our present translation calls it "the sound of a gentle breeze": other versions speak of "a still small voice". However we translate it, it involves a total contrast with the mayhem which has gone before, and it is there and then that Elijah meets God.

Transfer that to our own situation. Do you have times of upset, turmoil, and trouble in your life? Difficult times when you feel overwhelmed, at the mercy of circumstances, surrounded by things which you can't control? And can these not be compared to the gale, the earthquake and the fire which crash and burn around Elijah?

It isn't actually true to say that God is not in these things, in those times, in those circumstances. He is indeed in them, but we can't recognise His presence until some sort of calm returns; and then, if we are willing to reflect, if we are willing to be still and open, we can recognise that He is there, we can see what He was saying to us in the turmoil, we can grasp what He is asking of us now.

Of course, the danger is that, when calm returns, we simply breathe a sigh of relief and move on without reflecting, without giving God the time and space in which He invites us to meet Him; but if we are wise, we will imitate Elijah in taking our stand before the Lord, allowing ourselves to be drawn into a deeper encounter with Him, contemplating what He was saying to us in the turbulence, and what He is asking of us now.

Many many moons ago, our Pastoral Director in the seminary, the late Fr. Brian Green, use to insist on two things: experience and reflection on experience. In its way, that translates the Elijah episode into the here and now, as we listen to God in the light of events, and ponder His message in them.

Moving on to the Gospel, we find the apostles, like Elijah, caught up in a storm. Here, despite what the Old Testament writer has said, it is made clear that the Lord IS in the storm. Jesus, who walks on the lake in the eye of the storm, speaks from the storm and from the heart of their fears, and says "Courage! It is I. Do not be afraid."

Jesus, the living God, is at the heart of the turmoil which seems to threaten us: the thing which we fear is actually He. We are invited, like Peter, to step out of our comfort zone, to confront the things which disturb and frighten us, to walk across the water to Jesus who calls to us from the storm's epicentre to trust Him, who will not allow us to sink.

A few days ago, I was speaking to a priest recently released after a conviction which even the authorities recognise was unjust, and I asked him, "If at the time of your ordination, you had known what lay ahead, would you still have gone forward?"

He replied "Yes" because he had been able to recognise the presence of Christ in all the horror of his situation, and his priesthood had been worth preserving, and had been preserved, through it all. He had walked, however unwillingly, into the eye of the storm, and Christ had held him up.

"Courage! It is I. Do not be afraid." May we have the insight and the openness to hear Our Lord speaking those words to us in whatever storms we may encounter.

Reflection 33 — Is.56:1,6-7, Ps.66:2-3,5-6,8, Rom.11:13-15,29-32, Matt.15:21-28

No to anti-Semitism

What did I tell you? There are weeks like last week when there is almost too much in the readings to preach about, then there is this week which is a bit of a stinker. What are we to make of it?

At the heart of today's readings is the question of God's choice and call, and particularly of His choice of the Jewish people. They were the original people formed and called by God to receive His special favour, above all the favour of receiving His Son, God-made-man, the Word become flesh. Today's choice of readings calls us to consider where non-Jewish peoples fitted into God's plan, and where the Jews, and others, stand in relation to God's call today.

In the first place, the Book of Isaiah makes the point that God's call is not narrow. "Foreigners who have attached themselves to the Lord to serve Him and to love His name, and to be His servants—these I will bring to my holy mountain...for my house will be called a house of prayer for all the peoples."

The Jews of the prophet's time have suffered at the hands of the nations around them, but now that they have become re-established in their own land after their return from exile in Babylon, they are able to take a wider view of these nations, to recognise that God has a call for them too: that God is not a Jewish tribal god, but the one true God who wishes to gather both Jews and Gentiles to Himself.

That idea is present in the psalm as well: "All nations (will) learn your saving help...let ALL the peoples praise you". God has chosen the Jewish people, but they are the first fruits, and the non-Jewish nations are to follow.

But when? That question lies behind Jesus' encounter with the Canaanite woman. Our Lord at first refuses to answer the woman, not because He is some sort of racist, or misogynist, but because He has been sent to the Jewish people. As He understands His mission, it is not yet time for Him to build God's Kingdom among non-Jews, just as it was not time for Him to reveal His glory at the marriage-feast at Cana.

Yet, just as at Cana, where His mother drew His attention to the embarrassment of a pair of newly-weds, so here, Jesus cannot resist faith-filled prayer, and He goes outside the confines of His mission to fulfil the woman's request. There are two points to consider there: earnest prayer does work, and God's salvation and His Kingdom will extend in due course beyond the original chosen people, the Jews.

By the time St. Paul was writing to the Christians in Rome, the whole question of Jews and Gentiles had changed radically. The Jewish religious and political establishment had rejected Jesus, and although the original disciples were drawn from among the Jewish people, by and large it was Gentiles rather than Jews who accepted the Gospel.

So where did this leave the Jews? This is the question over which we found Paul agonising last week. This week we can almost feel his relief as he works out the answer to his problem. The answer is that the Jewish people can be left in God's hands. Their rejection of Jesus was all part of God's plan, to enable the Gentiles to be brought into God's Kingdom. Once the Gentiles have come in, God will bring in the Jews, as a people, in His own way and in His own time.

Paul realised this in the space of a couple of chapters, yet it has taken the world, and the Church, practically 2,000 years to catch up with his teaching. Dreadful crimes have been committed against the Jews throughout history, and the Church has been as much to blame as the rest of the world. Arguably, it was only the unprecedented horror of the Holocaust during the Second World War which forced the Church to examine its attitude, and it was not until the document "Nostra Aetate" of the Second Vatican Council that the Church officially and definitively rejected anti-Semitism, and repudiated the notion that the Jewish people as a whole could be held responsible for the death of Christ. The Council made clear that to claim that Jews today can be blamed for the killing of Christ is heresy.

Interestingly, Pope Benedict XVI, in his recent trilogy, "Jesus of Nazareth", spells the position out even more clearly. The Pope emeritus writes "We realise today with horror how many misunderstandings with grave consequences have weighed down our history" and he draws on St. Paul to make the point that we are not in the business of converting Jews. "Israel" he says, "is in the hands of God, who will save it "as a whole" at the proper time, when the number of Gentiles is complete". (Volume 2 page 46).

In the meantime, let us pray earnestly that hatred and violence carried out in the name of God may come to an end.

Reflection 34 **Is.22:19-23, Ps.137:1-3,6,8, Rom.11:33-36, Matt.16:13-20**

There are answers and answers

Have I told you about coefficients of expansion? The problem is that, having been here just over six years, I am now onto the third time around for this set of readings, and I can't always remember what I said last time they came around, or the time before.

Anyway, on the grounds that you probably can't remember either, I am going to mention coefficients of expansion. They cropped up in physics lessons many, many moons ago, and one day, for homework, we were given a whole set of problems involving them. Now it just so happened that the answers to the problems were given in the back of the textbook, and some enterprising lads in my form simply turned to the back of the book and copied down the answer.

And guess what? They didn't get any marks. Why not? Because it wasn't enough to give the answer: you had to show the working out.

I always think of that when I hear Our Lord's question to the disciples at Caesarea Philippi—and not just at Caesarea Philippi, but here and now to you and me—"Who do you say that I am?"

We know the answer to that: we have known it all our lives. We don't even need to look in the back of the book. Just like Peter, we can stick up a hand and say "You are the Christ, the Son of the living God".

So do we get full marks? No. Why not? Because we have to show the working out. All right then. What if we take it a bit further? What if we say that Peter gave this answer on behalf of the Church, because he was about to be appointed its leader, and that the Pope is his successor and speaks on behalf of the Church today? And perhaps we will go further still, and add that "Petros"—"Peter"—is the masculine form of "petra" the Greek word for rock, and that Our Lord was using a clever play on words. And let's go even further than that, and point to Peter's role of binding and loosing, and his possession of the keys of the Kingdom. Can we have full marks now?

Unfortunately, the answer is still "No". All of that is correct, and it is very praiseworthy that you should know it, but it is what we might call "head knowledge". It might get us full marks if we were dealing with coefficients of expansion—though whether St. Peter had anything to do with coefficients of expansion I am not entirely sure—but when we are dealing with the Christ, the Son of the living God, the working out has to be done not just in our heads, or even on paper, but in our lives.

To say that Jesus is the Christ has implications for the way we live. Last Monday's Gospel, also from St. Matthew, made that clear. It was the story of the rich young man who came to Jesus and asked how to obtain eternal life. "Keep the commandments" was the answer. "Done that! What else is there?" And Jesus spelt it out in full: "Sell what you own, give the money to the poor, and come, follow me."

What Jesus asked of the young man, what He asks of us, because He is the Christ, the Son of the living God, is nothing less than ourselves. He doesn't simply ask for head knowledge, which we can provide in answer to His question. He doesn't ask only for the answer of obedience, which the young man had given up to that point. He asks for the answer of love: He asks for the gift of ourselves.

Peter, the Pope, the Church, are all given to us to bring us closer to Christ, to help us to live out more fully the implications of the answer to His question, but we must always remember that they are means to the end, and not the end itself. The end is union with Jesus the Christ, the Son of the living God, and our working out of that union is our whole life's task.

Reflection 35   Jer.20:7-9, Ps.62:2-6,8-9, Rom.12:1-2, Matt.16:21-27

Tell me what you want

"Tell me what you want, what you really really want." Do you realise, it is around twenty years since the Spice Girls became famous? Did they get what they wanted, what they really really wanted? I suppose that Posh Spice wanted David Beckham, so that worked out, but what about DB himself? Like many sportsmen he has found it difficult to leave the field of play, carrying on to the last possible moment. And then there is "Freddie" Flintoff, turning out for Lancashire again five years after retiring: you sense in Freddie a permanent restlessness, a need to be playing sport long after his body has told him to pack it in.

What about the rest of us? What do you want, do you really really want? And have you got it? As a lad, I wanted to be grown-up, and especially to have left school, so that there would no longer be people making me do what I didn't want to do. Well, I left school a long time ago, though I am not sure that I have ever grown up, and as for the other part of the equation, well it doesn't happen, does it, not least because we are not sure what we do or do not want to do?

Jeremiah the prophet wanted peace. Don't we all? Or at least we think we do. He wanted to stop having to prophesy in God's name, because it landed him in all sorts of trouble. Yet this was his vocation. As he said elsewhere, the Lord chose him before he was born, and every time he tried to abandon his role as a prophet, something deep inside him drove him on. "There seemed to be a fire burning in my heart, imprisoned in my bones. The effort to restrain it wearied me: I could not bear it."

At one level, Jeremiah wanted to stop, but at a deeper level was a desire amounting to a compulsion to continue doing God's will.

What was this desire? According to the Psalm it was a longing for God, a longing which dwells deep within the human heart, whether we are aware of it or not.

"O God, you are my God, for you I long. For you my soul is thirsting, my body pines for you, like a dry weary land without water."

The psalmist is saying that what we want, what we really really want, is actually God, and that nothing else can satisfy us. All our other longings, our yearnings, even our lusts, are expressions of this desire for God, and for union with that God from whom we are sprung, and to whom we are destined to return. Centuries later, St. Augustine of

Hippo expressed the same conviction in his famous prayer: "You have made us for yourself, O Lord, and our hearts are restless till they rest in you."

St. Paul too makes the same point when he calls on the Christians in Rome to "let your behaviour change, modelled by your new mind" and when he speaks of "what is good, what it is that God wants, what is the perfect thing to do", the implication being that what God wants is what, deep down, we want too, whether or not we realise it.

Actually, it is intriguing that Paul speaks of "what... God wants" as if God too might answer the Spice Girls' question. What does God want, does He really really want? God wants us to be in union with Him.

(Interestingly enough, four hundred years before Christ, the Greek philosophers, Socrates and Plato, reached a similar conclusion through their analysis of virtue and their concept of the Form of the Good, but if you want to get home for tea/dinner, we had better not follow that track.)

Yet, although at the deepest level, our desire is for God, the fulfilment of that desire doesn't come easily. For Our Lord it involved going to Jerusalem, suffering grievously, being put to death. No wonder that when Peter, with the best of intentions, tried to dissuade Him, Jesus felt this as a real temptation, and recognised the wiles of Satan, speaking with the voice of His friend. (Incidentally, this incident flags up the nature and the limits of papal infallibility: when the Pope is inspired by God, as when Peter proclaimed Jesus as the Christ, he is infallible. When he follows his own instincts, he is as prone to mistakes as the rest of us.)

For the Son of God, the desire for God entailed suffering and death, and He warns us that, for us as well, it will involve taking up the Cross. "Anyone who wants to save his/her life will lose it, but anyone who loses that life for my sake will find it." Sometimes we have to give up what we think we want, the desire of the moment, for what we truly want, that union with God, the desire for which may be buried very deep, but which is the true source of all our desires. "Tell me what you want, what you really really want." We want God, and, in the last analysis, nothing else will do.

Reflection 36

Ez.33:7-9, Ps.94:1-2,6-9, Rom.13:8-10, Matt.18:15-20

Who wants a fight?

"Fight! Fight! Fight!" Do you remember the cry which used to go up in the playground if two lads were having a set-to? People would rush up and form a circle around them until a teacher or prefect waded in and hauled them off for summary retribution.

That was lads. Lasses were something else. The things they would do with fingernails and handfuls of hair had to be seen to be believed. In adult life, I have once or twice intervened to try to separate pugilistic lads, but I value my life too highly to get into the firing line if lasses are having a ding-dong.

I presume that is NOT what Our Lord had in mind when He told the disciples "Go and have it out with him alone, between your two selves". I take it that He is speaking about verbal fraternal correction, though, as I have said before, I think that it would have done St. Paul a world of good if Peter had given him a good smack in the mouth when he was coming over all superior and smug about Peter's failure of nerve in the matter of eating with the Gentile converts.

What Jesus is speaking about appears to be the need for correction within the community, and about the importance, and indeed the power, of that community. In the 1970s, "community" became a buzz word within the Church—what I would call a Crackerjack word, after the Children's TV programme Crackerjack in which, every time the word "Crackerjack" was mentioned, everyone had to shout it back, and become all excited. People did the same with the word "community". In my seminary days, a few people used to bang on about the importance of community: ironically, they were always the people who couldn't get on with anybody else.

But, as they say around Bleasdale, "abusus non tollit usum"—just because people make a mess of an idea, it doesn't make the idea invalid. The community of the Church is a powerful and important concept. Again in the seventies, people would say "The Church used to be a fortress, and now it is a community" forgetting that "community" is Latin for "fortress", "communitus" meaning "fortified together". A genuine community has the strength of a fortress, and when the Church is united in love, it has power even with God, for Christ is at the heart of it: "Where two or three meet in my name, I shall be there with them".

Yet the walls of a fortress can develop cracks, and the cracks in the fortress, or community, of the Church in recent years have been not so much failures of belief or orthodoxy, though these are not unimportant, but failures of charity, of fraternity, of sorority. "See these Christians, how they love one another", the exclamation attributed to pagans by Tertullian in the second century, has often been a hollow claim.

Instead of the fraternal correction, the strength-filled guidance, of the offender, for which Jesus calls, there has been too much infighting, too many mutual recriminations, too much desire to see the other person put down. Too often, the Church has resembled the lads scrapping in the playground, or even that much rougher element, the lasses.

The Ezekiels in positions of authority have, at times, taken too much pleasure in threatening those whom they regard as sinners, and, in return, there has been an excessive eagerness to shove up two fingers at the wielders of power. The community, or fortress, of the Church, should not be a setting behind whose walls people are at each other's throats, or a base from which the cavalry rides out to launch punitive raids on those outside.

Instead, it should be a source of mutual strength, giving us the assurance of support and the confidence to engage charitably with those outside, to welcome them into a setting where they too are at home. And this needs to begin where we are, in the parish. Is the parish a setting of mutual love and support? Is this church a place in which outsiders would recognise the presence of Christ—would be able to sense that Christ is here because you have gathered?

Please God it is, but there will always be room for improvement. We will always need to examine our consciences, to ask ourselves whether our thoughts, words, and actions are always rooted in Christ's own love for our fellow-parishioners, and then more widely for our fellow-Catholics, our fellow Christians, our fellow human beings. As the prophets suggest, as Christ states, there may always be need for fraternal correction, but let it be always truly fraternal, and let it begin with a willingness to correct ourselves.

Reflection 37 Num.21:4-9, Ps.77:1-2,34-38, Phil.2:6-11, Jn.3:13-17

The bite of the serpent

Have you been bitten by a serpent recently? There are a lot of them about. There is the serpent of jealousy, the serpent of gossip, the serpent of malice, the serpent of rage, the serpent of lying, which disguises itself as the harmless little serpent of "white lies which don't matter", the serpent of foul language, the serpent of lust, the serpent of apathy, the serpent of selfishness and self-centredness, the serpent of sloth, the serpent of judgmentalism, the serpent of hard-heartedness, and that serpent which is said to be the most deadly of them all, the serpent of discouragement.

That last serpent, the serpent of discouragement, seems to be very busy in the diocese at the moment. A lot of good priests seem to have been bitten, and to have become downhearted, tired, run down; and that can lead to the danger of becoming cynical. And that's another serpent which bites a lot of people today—the serpent of cynicism which, as it bites you, whispers in your ear that THEY are all alike: they are all on the make; they can't be trusted; you may as well pack the whole thing in."

As I say, there are a lot of serpents about; and so I ask again, "Have you been bitten by a serpent recently?"

And if you have, did you find a bronze serpent, which you could look at, and so live? Because, make no mistake, the bite of many of these serpents is deadly. You may go on breathing, moving, speaking, but inwardly, if you are bitten by the serpent of malice, apathy, cynicism, and so on, you will be dead or dying.

And so that is another question which I will repeat: did you find a bronze serpent, which you could look at, and so live? Did you talk to someone, read something, watch something, ponder something, which would help to cure you of the deadly bite of those serpents? Did you manage to overcome all the negative stuff, all that was Discouraging, so as to find genuine and deep Encouragement? Did you take your snake bites to the confessional to expose them to the searing, healing, sacramental love of God, so that the words of the priest, and the power of the sacrament, could drive out the poison from your system?

That last question is bound up with the ultimate question: did you recognise, working through and beyond the bronze serpent, the ultimate healer whom the bronze serpent represents, namely Jesus the Christ, lifted up on the Cross, sent into the world for that very purpose, to be lifted up as the healing of every bite of every evil serpent which seeks to destroy your life?

Did you realise that the crucified Christ is the antidote to all negativity, and the source of all that is positive, uplifting, healing? Did you turn to Him directly in prayer, in adoration, and did you find His presence in the various bronze serpents which helped you overcome those negative bites?

Ponder that last sentence of today's Gospel: "God sent His Son into the world, not to condemn the world, but so that, through Him, the world might be saved". Those words contain the antidote to all negativity: the vision of Christ, lifted up on the Cross, puts all cynicism to flight.

Have you been bitten by a serpent recently? If you have, make use of the various bronze serpents which God sends you, and recognise in them the presence of Christ crucified, whose healing love is more powerful than the most deadly of any serpent's bites.

Reflection 38 **Is.55:6-9, Ps.144:2-3,8-9,17-18, Phil.1:20-24,27, Matt.20:1-16**

What time is it?

Time is passing, and you don't need me to tell you that it seems to pass more quickly all the time. I had a reminder a week or so ago when I conducted a wedding. The groom had mentioned his Cambridge College, and I had a very clear memory of refereeing an excellent game involving that college two or three weeks, or months, or years ago, only of course it wasn't: it was forty four years ago, long before either the groom or the bride was thought of.

Time is passing, and all of us are at different hours of the day, from the first to the eleventh. Are we labouring in the Lord's vineyard, and if that feels like too big a question for the moment, are we seeking the Lord, as Isaiah puts it? Are we calling to him?

"Of course we are," you may say, "otherwise we wouldn't be here". Fair point. But is this simply our weekly nod to God, or are we genuinely seeking Him throughout our week and throughout our lives, opening our hearts and minds to Him each day, trying to discern what He wants of us, today and throughout our earthly span?

This is a question for me, as much as it is for you. I might try to claim that I have been labouring in the Lord's vineyard for decades, but I still need to examine my conscience every day, to ask myself whether I still have the same zeal and enthusiasm which drove me as a young priest, whether I am working in the right way, and at the right tasks, whether I am truly responding to the Lord's call every day, or simply ambling along with my own agenda.

And another question: do I, do you, in any way resemble the first hour workers who make comparisons, who think that they are entitled to more recognition than others? In the terms of the actual parable, we are all ELEVENTH hour workers, because we are Gentiles who have come late to the workforce after the Jewish people have borne the heat and burden of the day; but we quickly forget that, and quickly promote ourselves to an imagined prominence from which we can look down on others.

Pope Francis, it seems, has been on the receiving end of that kind of resentment, as he is attempting to reform the Church, to make it more Christ-like. One cardinal in Rome was quoted as saying "Who does this Argentinian think he is?" Er, well, I think he thinks he is the Pope, who has been chosen to be Chief Shepherd on earth of the flock of the Good Shepherd, and who is calling his fellow-shepherds, in his own words, "to live with the smell of the sheep".

Recently, an American bishop delivered a lecture in which he commented that some of his brother-bishops in the US don't like Francis, because he is shaking them up, questioning the way they have been doing things, pushing them out of their comfort zones. Over time, we all find our comfort zones, our own way of working, our own way of serving, which can easily become a way of self-serving, and like the bolshie foreman of the parable we can object to what we perceive as a threat.

If we have any sense, we shall see Pope Francis, not as a threat, but as an encouragement, and as a challenge. He is encouraging us, and challenging us, to see other people as Christ sees them, and to see ourselves as the less than profitable workers that we are, in need always of the rich forgiveness of which Isaiah speaks.

Francis is able to do this because he is aware of his own serious failings, because he knows that he has no right to claim any sort of moral superiority, as the first hour workers tried to claim it. Pope Francis knows, and has admitted, that as the Provincial Superior of the Jesuits when he was in his thirties, he made serious errors which divided the order, and failed people who were suffering at the hands of the military government.

It is his sense of his own weakness, his own failures and, as he readily admits, his own sins, which enables the Pope to be compassionate with the weaknesses, the failures, the sins of others. I heard recently of a priest in Scotland who asked for prayers for, as he put it, "our very lax Pope". I can only assume that this same priest would have condemned Jesus for laxity in His encounter with the woman taken in adultery, and with other sinners. Perhaps when Jesus responded "Let him who is without sin cast the first stone" this priest would have grabbed the nearest rock. (Incidentally, I also wonder whether this non-lax priest spends two hours per day in prayer before the Blessed Sacrament, as Francis does.)

Personally, I would rather stand with Francis, recognising my own sinfulness, realising that, however many years have passed, I am still, at best, an eleventh hour worker, seeking the Lord while He is still to be found, calling to Him while He is still near. What about you?

Reflection 39 — Ez.18:25-28, Ps.24:4-9, Phil.2:1-11, Matt.21:28-32

To be the same as Christ Jesus

"In your minds, you must be the same as Christ Jesus." Oh heck! Am I? Are you? Am I heck as like. Are you heck as like. What would it involve? St. Paul spells it out: total self-emptying in love, giving up His status, giving up His life, all in self-abandoning love for an ungrateful human race. Are we even slightly like that? Maybe. Maybe not. Probably much more unlike than like.

Can we improve? Can we make progress? Both Ezekiel and Our Lord suggest that we can—but that we can also go the other way. The prophet talks about the good man who goes wrong, and the bad man who reforms: Jesus has the parable of the two sons.

Looking over the readings, I immediately thought of AA Milne's poem about Good Bear and Bad Bear.

"There were two little bears who lived in a wood, and one of them was bad, and the other was good.

Good Bear learned his twice times one--but Bad Bear left all his buttons undone.

And then quite suddenly (just like us) one got better, and the other got wuss."

I remember my former university chaplain comparing two students who lodged at the chaplaincy to Good Bear and Bad Bear, one of them always on time for lectures (and for Mass) with all his work done punctually, while the other was constantly sleeping in; and how they both suddenly underwent a complete reversal. So that sort of thing does happen.

Our Lord's parable, on the other hand, makes me think of Jim. Jim was in my form in my first year after ordination, when I was on the staff of the now defunct Junior Seminary. One week, in the course of that year, the headmaster, Fr. O'Neill, was principal celebrant at Mass for the junior forms, and that parable of the two sons cropped up one day as the Gospel. "Now," said Fr. O'Neill, "you have heard that story of the son who says that he won't go to work, and yet goes, and of the other son who says that he will go, and doesn't. Now there is a third possibility. What is that?"

And some bright eyed, bushy tailed youth put up his hand and said "He could say that he will go, and then go".

"Very good," said Fr. O'Neill, but straightaway, there was Jim, hand shooting aloft. "Father," he gasped out, "there is a fourth one. He could have said he wouldn't go, and not have gone."

Fr. O'Neill withered him with a look. "I don't think we need to consider that" came the reply, while I was thinking "Oh heck. That's the one I was thinking of. The third one never occurred to me."

Thirty eight years on, I wonder whether Jim might have had a better insight into human psychology than Fr. O'Neill. The immediately dutiful son (whom, let's face it, Jesus doesn't consider) may be too good to be true. The faultless person who invariably says and does the right thing seems to lack an element of humanity. After all, consider the Son of God Himself, and what an awkward so-and-so He was as a twelve year old, going missing for three days, and then responding to his parents' anxieties with a typically juvenile shrug of the shoulders, and the equivalent of "Whatever". Which brings to mind a homily during my first term in seminary, as Fr. Tony Pearson of the Leeds Diocese recalled the advice given by his parish priest as the young Anthony Pearson was about to embark on his own seminary training:

"Now, Tony," said the parish priest, "when you go to Ushaw, there'll be lots of things you've got to do, and lots of things you've not got to do, and if you do all the things you've got to do, and you don't do all the things you've not got to do, then they'll make you a bishop. AND TONY, YOU'LL BE NO BLOODY GOOD."

Instant perfection, unquestioning adherence to the rules, should be viewed with suspicion. The first son in the parable, overcoming his reluctance and coming to obedience with a struggle, is likely to be more reliable in the long run than Fr. O'Neill's imaginary third son for whom conformity presents no problem.

The time will come in all our lives when doing God's will provides a challenge, and we will meet that challenge far better if we have struggled along the way. After all, the ultimate challenge is to be "the same as Christ Jesus" and that will involve a lifelong struggle.

Reflection 40 Is.5:1-7, Ps.79:9,12-16,19-20, Phil.4:6-9, Matt.21:33-43

What do you know about vines?

This week's readings are a bit worrying. They remind me that I have to tread carefully; to remember that I am a townie living in the country; to be careful that I don't put my foot in things (and you know what kind of things you can put your foot in in the country).

Actually, I am becoming quite countrified. I can look at flowers and say "That's a red one, that's a yellow one, that's a blue one." I can look at animals and say "That's a sheep. That's a cow." But when it comes to vines, I know that I am in foreign territory; though perhaps I am not alone in that: I may be mistaken, but I don't think that viticulture is a huge industry, even in Claughton.

It was a big thing in ancient Israel, though, and in Jewish culture and religion, vines and the fruit of the vine had and have a large part to play. The Passover meal, the high point of Jewish religious life, involves a number of cups of wine, over one of which Jesus spoke the words of consecration whereby the wine became His blood which was to be poured out on Calvary for the cleansing and salvation of the world, and handed down to us in a perpetual "making present" of both meal and death.

For the author of today's psalm, the vine signified the whole people of Israel, transplanted from Egypt, set firm in the Promised Land, spreading throughout the countryside as far as the sea. Yet now, says the psalmist, the protecting wall of the vineyard has been broken down, and the vine which is Israel has become vulnerable, to be plucked, uprooted, and destroyed by all and sundry as the people suffer at the hands of their enemies.

"Why has this happened? he asks, yet the final verse suggests that he knows the answer. "We shall never forsake you again" is the psalm's promise to God, indicating that the people have indeed forsaken God, and that this is the reason for their current misfortunes.

That is spelt out even more clearly by Isaiah, who claims that the beloved vine, which is God's people, has produced sour grapes, and who goes on to foretell the very sufferings which the psalm laments: the vine will be trampled on, ruined, despoiled, precisely because the people have failed to respond to God's love, have not produced the fruit which God was entitled to expect. And in case we are in any doubt at all, the prophet is explicit: "The vineyard of the Lord of hosts is the House of Israel and the men of Judah that chosen plant. He expected justice, but found bloodshed; integrity, but only a cry of distress."

So by the time of Jesus, those who heard Him would have been quick to pick up on the concept of Israel as the vine, as it was part of their religious heritage; and when He echoed Isaiah's description of the winepress and the tower, they would have been on familiar territory.

Our Lord, though, in His telling of the parable, makes a couple of subtle changes from Isaiah. The vineyard and its vines are now identified with the Kingdom of God, rather than with the nation of Israel; and the villains of the piece are no longer the unfruitful vine, but the tenants who have custody of the vineyard. They kill, first the prophets, who are depicted as servants of God, the vineyard owner, and finally the owner's son, clearly Jesus Himself, and the outcome of their misdeeds is not, as in Isaiah and the psalm, the destruction of the vineyard and its contents, but the punishment of the murderous tenants, who represent the religious leaders and the handing over of the vineyard (the Kingdom) to new tenants (the Gentiles).

So far, so good. We may be inclined as Gentiles, as the Church, as inheritors of the Kingdom, to take comfort from this whole series of parables. But caution is needed. Sauce for the goose is sauce for the gander. What was demanded of the Jewish people is equally demanded of us, and we have to ask ourselves whether our record, both as individuals and as the Church, is any better than theirs.

The paedophile scandals in the Church are surely as bad as, if not worse than, anything perpetrated by the leaders of the original chosen people, and can we honestly claim that, in the manner of our lives, we are bearing the fruit which God is entitled to expect? We have no grounds for complacency. Our Lord's promise was precisely that the Kingdom would be given to a people that would produce its fruit. What kind of fruit are you and I bearing?

Reflection 41

Apoc.7:2-4,9-14, Ps.23:1-6, 1 Jn.3:1-3, Matt.5:1-12

Remember, remember...

November has been called the kindest month, because it is the month in which we remember. All Saints is followed by All Souls, by Remembrance Sunday and Armistice Day, and we can even throw in Bonfire Night for good measure: Remember, remember, the fifth of November... Indeed the whole month is given up to remembering, and to praying for, those who have gone before us.

Is this simply an exercise in nostalgia or, to put it more kindly, in entertaining good thoughts, or is there something here of greater importance? To remember is, literally, to re-member, to put the members, or limbs, back together, and that is what the Church invites us to do, at all times of the year, but especially in this, the year's penultimate month.

We are, as St. Paul impressed upon us, members, or limbs, of Christ's body, the Church; and not only we, but all those who have gone before us, throughout the ages and throughout the world, members of Christ and of one another, joined in a unity which cannot be severed even by death. When we remember, we consciously reunite ourselves with one another, and especially with the dead, who are alive to God and to us, and that reuniting has its positive, practical effect in prayer, as we seek the prayers of our departed fellow-members, and we offer effective prayer for them, that their unity with God, their perfection as members of Christ, may be complete.

And so our prayer is the active, vital, positive part of our re-membering, strengthening us as the body of Christ, building more firmly our unity with the world-wide, time-wide, eternity-wide Church, reinforcing our mutual support.

By holding two separate feasts of All Saints and All Souls, we distinguish those whose need for perfection to bring them into complete unity with God is complete—the saints—from those whom we call the Holy Souls, for whom that perfection is still a work in progress; yet in reality, the two feasts are part of one whole. Whilst there are some whom the Church has officially named as saints, for the vast majority of the dead we cannot know exactly how they stand before God. In any case, the question is an artificial one, brought on by our tendency always to think in terms of time, and to view eternity as a long, long, ever-so-long time, whereas it is a different dimension altogether.

What is clear, both from the scriptures, and from our own experience, reason, and logic, is that everyone who has ever lived, with the exception of Jesus Our Lord, and of His

Blessed Mother, who was preserved by His merits from every stain of sin—everyone else has needed/needs/will need that cleansing, perfecting, purifying which we call purgatory, and therefore both needs and offers to us that beautiful gift of mutual support which is prayer.

If we were in any doubt about that, today's Second Reading should banish those doubts. "What we are to be in the future has not yet been revealed" says St. John. "All we know is that, when it is revealed, we shall be like God, because we shall see Him as He really is."

To see God as He really is: what an awesome experience that will be, at once both glorious and terrifying. What effect will that have on us? It will make us like God, says St. John. Are you like God? Are you heck as like, any more than I am. Well, perhaps a bit more than I am, but still not like God. How will we become like God? By a change so drastic, so dramatic, so mind-boggling, that we cannot even begin to imagine it. What is the one thing which we know about change? That it is painful. Birth, childhood, adolescence, adulthood, midlife, old age, death: none of these changes takes place without pain—we even have a saying "No pain, no gain"—so the change to become like God will inevitably bring the sharpest pain of all, and that pain will be purgatory, our purging, our purifying, our perfecting, a pain which will nonetheless be welcome, because we shall already have seen our glorious goal. As the late Fr. Vincent Smith put it: "Purgatory will be seeing God, and realising that we are not fit to be seen".

What form that purgatory will take, nobody knows, as St. John points out. The lurid pictures conjured up in the Middle Ages, which caused some of the more extreme Reformers to throw out the baby of Purgatory with the bath water of the imagery, were simply an attempt to picture the unpictureable, to give the mind something to hold onto. Nor does it matter. What truly matters is our unity in the one body with all those who have gone before us, and our concern for mutual support, as we seek the helping prayers of the saints and Holy Souls, without worrying too much about who falls into which category, and offer the help of our prayers. Thus our remembering becomes truly a re-membering, and November is genuinely the kindest month.

Reflection 42   Ez.47:1-2,8-9,12, Ps.45:2-3,5-6,8-9, 1 Cor.3:9-11,16-17, Jn.2:13-22

The Lateran Basilica? Eh?

What's this in aid of then? What on earth is the Lateran Basilica when it's at home, and why is it considered so important that it displaces the Sunday liturgy?

The Lateran Basilica, often called St. John Lateran, is the church of St. John on the Lateran Hill in Rome, and one of the four great Roman basilicas, the others being St. Peters, on the Vatican Hill, St. Mary Major, and St Paul's-outside-the-walls. Perhaps most significantly, it is the Pope's Cathedral as Bishop of Rome, a title on which Pope Francis lays particular emphasis.

So today's feast emphasises the unity of the Church in communion with, and under the leadership of, the Bishop of Rome: it is the feast which reminds us that we are Catholics. What then do the scripture readings suggest as to how we should celebrate this feast?

All three readings speak about the Temple, the Temple which was built of stones, and the Temple which is Christ's body, both literally, and figuratively as the Church of which we are the members. There then is the first clue: this feast has something to do with the building which is the basilica, but also with the people who are joined in unity as members of Christ's body, the Church.

So far, so good. Let's push on then, to consider the readings individually. The prophet Ezekiel was writing during the exile of the Jewish people to Babylon. He had a vision of the Jerusalem Temple, which the Babylonians had destroyed, rebuilt and restored to its former glory, as indeed it was to be. His chief emphasis, though, is on the life-giving water flowing out of the Temple.

Detective work under weigh: bells ringing. "Ah" you will say, "Today's Gospel tells us that Jesus' body is the true Temple, destroyed and rebuilt; and elsewhere, St. John speaks of the Holy Spirit as streams of living water flowing from the heart of Christ. Also, it is St. John who describes the soldier piercing the side of Christ as He hung upon the Cross, bringing forth blood and water which are seen as representing the blood of the Eucharist and the water of baptism. So Ezekiel's vision finds its fulfilment in Christ." (That is what you were thinking, isn't it?)

So put all that together, and we have the Temple, which is Christ, and which is the Church, as the source of living and life-giving water, which are both baptism and the ongoing outpouring of the Holy Spirit. How does this tie in with St. John Lateran? That

SYMBOLISES the Church, the body of Christ, gathered in unity by the Pope, the Bishop of Rome.

Let's move on to St. Paul. He begins by saying "YOU are God's building", but not just any building. "You are God's Temple and... the Spirit of God is living *en humin*" here translated as "among you" but better rendered as "in you". So Jesus is the Temple of God, but because we are in Jesus, because we are His body, then WE are the Temple of God. What does it mean to say that we are the Temple of God? Well, the Temple is where God dwelt, so St. Paul is saying that God dwells in us, both individually because of our baptism, and collectively because we are the Church.

Are we making progress? I think so. Let's push on then to the Gospel. It begins with Our Lord purifying the Temple. So we must ensure that we allow Him to purify us as the Temple of God, to drive from us everything which is not compatible with living His life, but also that we ask Him to do the same for the Church as a whole.

More than that, scholars say that St. John sees Our Lord as overturning Temple worship in itself, replacing it by focus on Him, the new and true Temple. That should remind us to be careful where we place our devotion—that it is on the person of Christ. We do not worship the Pope, or the Church, or particular buildings, but only Christ and His Father in the power of the Holy Spirit. The Pope, the Church, church buildings, are not unimportant, but their importance comes from their role in leading us to Christ. They are important as means to the end, and the end is union with Christ and the establishment of His Kingdom. In the last analysis, that is the point of this feast, that is the point of the Lateran Basilica, that is the point of the Pope and our unity under his leadership: the point of it all is Christ. (Are we more or less sorted?)

Reflection 43 **Ez.34:11-12,15-17, Ps.22:1-3,5-6, 1 Cor.15:20-26,28, Matt.25:31-46**

Ye ken the noo!

The story is told of the fire and brimstone preacher in the highlands who was waxing eloquent on the subject of the Last Judgement. As he reached the climax of his sermon, he thumped the pulpit and bellowed "And it will be no use saying—but Lord, we didna ken—because the Lord will reply—Well, ye ken the noo!"

That is a fair summary of Our Lord's parable of judgement which provides our Gospel reading this year on the Feast of Christ the King. In some ways, it is a slightly unfortunate Feast, established, as I have mentioned before, in the 1930s, as Pope Pius XI's response to the demands of fascism and state communism to establish a total claim on people's loyalty. Only Christ, replied the Pope, has such a claim, but in using the already outmoded concept of kingship, he risked the Feast being dismissed as an irrelevance in the modern world. As the old song didn't quite put it: "Kings ain't what they used to be."

Yet if we look at the Gospel passages chosen for the three years of the liturgical cycle, we can see a deeper meaning to our celebration. Next year, we shall hear Pontius Pilate questioning Our Lord about the nature of His kingship, and receiving the reply "My Kingdom is not of this world"; in two years' time, St. Luke will describe Jesus, the King who reigned from a cross, wearing a crown of thorns; and today we are told that the King will mount the throne of judgement only after sharing the lowliest and most painful aspects of the human condition, appearing to us hungry, thirsty, naked, a stranger, an invalid, and a prisoner.

Do we see the face of Christ the King in those who suffer? Really, that isn't the question. As Christ the Judge tells the story, the just no less than the damned are likely to say "But Lord, we didna ken". Perhaps it is a blessed thing to recognise the Suffering Saviour in His suffering people, but the more important thing is to serve Him whether we recognise Him or not.

You may know the story of St. Francis and the leper. As a young man, Francis was extremely fastidious, and had a particular horror of lepers. The story is told that, as Francis was riding out one day, a leper approached him, begging for alms. Although he was almost gagging with nausea, Francis forced himself to dismount, to embrace the leper, and to kiss him, before changing clothes with him, giving the leper his own rich apparel and riding away in rags. One version of the story adds that, a few yards down the road, Francis turned and looked back, and the leper was no longer there. "Then," muses the pious commentator, "Francis realised that the leper had been Christ." Well, maybe. The point is that the leper was, and always will be, Christ, whether Francis, or we, recognise Him or not.

The philosopher Blaise Pascal, said that "Christ is in agony to the end of time", suffering whenever and wherever His people suffer. Our task, as today's Gospel makes clear, is to relieve that suffering as best we can. How do we go about it?

In some ways, the hungry and thirsty Christ is the easiest to meet. We have regular collections and appeals on His behalf to which we can respond, though it is worth noting that the hungry Christ is beginning to reappear in our own towns and cities, making new demands on our generosity.

What about Christ the stranger? He may be someone as undramatic as a newcomer to the neighbourhood, or a new parishioner, a new pupil in school, a new workmate, perhaps needing nothing more than a smile or a friendly word. He may be someone who looks different, and therefore threatening. Again, a genuine smile can do much to disarm a threat which is likely to be more imaginary than real.

Perhaps, though, the Christ whom we encounter—or fail to encounter, as the case may be—most frequently, will be the sad and lonely Christ for whom a visit may be a great source of healing. In some ways, this can be the most elusive Christ, precisely because He is out of sight, and therefore out of mind.

This Christ may take the form of a family member who is concealing the rough time that s/he is passing through; a fellow-parishioner who is less mobile at present, whether temporarily or permanently; a shy person who finds mixing difficult. Visiting that person may be a joy for us—or it may be an unwelcome chore. That is not the point. A priest friend of mine sometimes raises the question "Whose needs are being met here?" In other words, are we somewhat selfishly trying to make ourselves feel good, or do we genuinely have the needs of the other person at heart? The suffering, sad, sick, lonely Christ may not give our ego a boost: that does not give us the right to ignore Him.

> **Maybe a question to ponder: is there someone whom I should phone, text, email, or visit at this time, someone who would benefit from such contact, whatever I may feel about it? That person may be Christ, and if, at the Last Judgement, I find myself saying "But Lord, I didna ken" let it be because I served Him, not because I overlooked Him.**

More Books!

I want morebooks!

Buy your books fast and straightforward online - at one of the world's fastest growing online book stores! Environmentally sound due to Print-on-Demand technologies.

Buy your books online at
www.get-morebooks.com

Kaufen Sie Ihre Bücher schnell und unkompliziert online – auf einer der am schnellsten wachsenden Buchhandelsplattformen weltweit! Dank Print-On-Demand umwelt- und ressourcenschonend produziert.

Bücher schneller online kaufen
www.morebooks.de

OmniScriptum Marketing DEU GmbH
Heinrich-Böcking-Str. 6-8
D - 66121 Saarbrücken
Telefax: +49 681 93 81 567-9

info@omniscriptum.com
www.omniscriptum.com

Scriptum

Printed by
Schaltungsdienst Lange o.H.G., Berlin